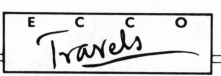

Smara: The Forbidden City by Michel Vieuchange
Italian Hours by Henry James

SMARA THE FORBIDDEN CITY

MICHEL VIEUCHANGE AT TIGILIT
AFTER HIS FIRST ATTEMPT

SMARA
THE FORBIDDEN CITY
Michel Vieuchange

Being the Journal of Michel Vieuchange while travel-
ing among the Independent Tribes of South
Morocco and Rio de Oro. Edited, with
Introduction and Epilogue, by Jean
Vieuchange. With a Preface by
Paul Claudel. Translated
from the French by
Fletcher Allen

▼

THE ECCO PRESS

NEW YORK

First published in 1932 by E.P. Dutton, New York
Published in 1987 by The Ecco Press
26 West 17th Street, New York, N.Y. 10011
Published simultaneously in Canada by
Penguin Books Canada Ltd., Ontario

Printed in the United States of America

Cover by Beth Tondreau Design

Library of Congress Cataloging-in-Publication Data

Vieuchange, Michel, 1904–1930.
Smara, the forbidden city.
(Ecco travels)
Translation of: Chez les dissidents
du Sud marocain et du Rio de Oro.
Reprint. Originally published: New York : E.P. Dutton, 1932.
Includes index.
1. Western Sahara—Description and travel.
2. Morocco—Description and travel.   3. Vieuchange,
Michel, 1904–1930—Journeys—Morocco.   4. Vieuchange,
Michel, 1904–1930—Journeys—Western Sahara.
I. Vieuchange, Jean.   II. Title.   III. Series.
DT346.S7V513   1987   916.4'804   87-6878
ISBN 0-88001-146-7

PREFACE

POVERTY has never lacked enthusiastic and faithful lovers since our Lord at His crucifixion gave her into the keeping of His beloved disciple, that he should receive her *in sua*.

The Pères Blancs, ministering in the desert, are her doorkeepers, night and day ; St. Francis became her knight, Don Quixote her standard-bearer. And in our own time—how well we remember them !—men of all nations found themselves so drawn to her that they enlisted in their millions under her banners and, forsaking all things—families, careers, even life itself—chose rather the privilege of eating the bitter bread of her cause and of sleeping in the mire at her side.

Even to-day, can it not be said that all the resources of science, of diplomacy, and of political economy have succeeded only in extending the boundaries of her kingdom to the uttermost ends of the earth ?

For many of her elect, no search is necessary to find her : they have no occasion to go beyond their own dwellings or their own country ; but for others, what labour, what effort ! It is surely for this pearl of the gospel that the wise merchant sells without hesitation all that he has.

Of such were Rembrandt, who withdrew the more when public favour sought him, finally to die with the hands of bailiffs seeking his throat ; Columbus, who discovered a new world, to bring back chains ; Napoleon, who conquered Europe, to assure himself possession of a rock in mid-Atlantic ; Rimbaud, eaten by cancer.

But never lover hastened to trysting-place at the bidding of his mistress with a heart so impatient, or in such complete abandonment, as this young man— whose journal of discovery and agony it is my task to introduce to the world—desired that place on the map, in the heart of inhuman solitude, whose almost invisible italics formed the two syllables : *Smara*.

Nothing dismayed him : fatigue, danger, hunger, thirst, coarse food, foul water, vermin, the sands and fires of Hell. He gave all his money, trusted himself, alone, to a few brigands whose language, even, he could not understand. He spent hours rolled in a bundle, tied hand and foot as an offering trussed for sacrifice. Baulked in a first endeavour, he began afresh, and succeeded. It was not too great a price to pay for the privilege of wandering for an hour or two in a village made of a few heaps of stones collected by nomads, and already deserted by them.

It was not too great a price, because his beloved kept her tryst. Yet, no sooner had he clambered into the

saddle of his camel, as to a throne of torture, no sooner
turned the muzzle of his ungainly beast to the north
than he knew the icy kiss on his lips and the chill that
pierced him to the marrow.

The journey he had made in a fervour of anticipation
he re-traced in agony, but mind and will were constantly awake in his unconquerable body, a body
ravaged by dysentery and shaken by the galling pace
of a beast itself almost dead. To the last moment,
compass, watch, and pencil noted the bearings of each
detail and deviation as the wilderness was crossed :
with a clear, steeled glance he dominated the strange
beings around him.

Reaching safety at last, he fell dying into the arms
of his brother : an aeroplane carried the spent victor
to his last bed. He alone knew what he had accomplished. He had fulfilled his destiny ; had given, in
one great effort, all that was asked of him : his heart's
blood, the quintessence of his intelligence and of his
will. More he could not have done. The moment
was at hand for him to receive his Lord.

*To him that overcometh, to him I will give of the
hidden manna, and I will give him a white stone.*[1]

That one for whom he had so hungered he embraced
at the end, and he knew that her promises were not
empty.

[1] *Revelation,* ii. 17.

He that hearkeneth to me shall not be confounded, And they that work by me shall not sin. They that explain me shall have life everlasting.[1]

PAUL CLAUDEL

WASHINGTON, *June 9, 1932*

---

[1] *Ecclesiasticus*, xxiv. 30, 31 (Douay version).

CONTENTS

SMARA THE FORBIDDEN CITY

SMARA : THE FORBIDDEN CITY

INTRODUCTION

BY

JEAN VIEUCHANGE

DURING the night of September 10–11, 1930, my brother Michel and I arrived by motor at the bank of the Oued [1] Massa, some twenty miles north of Tiznit, in south Morocco. There we had arranged to meet native guides, with whom my brother—disguised as a Berber woman—intended to penetrate the territory of the dissident tribes.

To-day, while I write this introduction, I live that moment again, a moment whose intensity was neither of joy nor of apprehension, but of haste. Action was imminent. My brother, stripping himself of his European clothes, put on a white robe and wrapped a thick veil round his face, a veil almost opaque, and whose effect was to muffle his voice. I can still visualize him, putting the cheap silver rings on to his fingers, and hanging the pendants which completed his disguise round his neck.

Then, our quick farewells over, he went off alone to the south, followed by his guides.

Michel was taking the first step in the dangerous

[1] River.

expedition which we had planned and matured together : to travel among the warlike, independent tribes of the Anti-Atlas and the Rio de Oro, and to make an attempt to reach Smara, the town of Ma el Aïnin, which, to that date had preserved its mystery.

For two months, my brother, a European, and alone, knowing neither Arabic nor Berber, lived among fanatical tribes jealous of their independence, and travelled on foot or by camel through a desert region, covering about nine hundred miles. He was finally able to reach his objective ; but, on the return journey, some days before reaching the French zone, was brought down by dysentery, and died at Agadir on November 30, 1930.

* * *

In organizing this expedition, we naturally did not fail to take into account the attendant dangers, but they did not lessen our enthusiasm ; rather, they fed it. But how can I now recount that enthusiasm, how avoid misrepresenting the joy we found in facing that action which really interpreted the attitude we then took to life ?

There was nothing in the constitution of my brother that would seem to lead him to an undertaking so arduous and so dangerous ; but, I know well enough that, after 1926, the course of his thoughts, his reading, discussions, and experiences laid the foundation.

That year, while completing his period of military service in Morocco, he ceased to believe in things that previously were dear to us. A childhood spent entirely in the provinces [1] with our family, a religious

[1] A year and a half older than myself, Michel was born at Nevers on August 26, 1904.

emphasis in early education, preparation first for his Bachelor's and then his Master's degree, a deep study of classical philology gave my brother a liking for meter and balance, and a classical sense of style. He admired Flaubert, Mistral, and the Greek poets.

Coming to Paris in 1922, although not disregarding the life of the streets, the activities of a great city, or the new surroundings in which he found himself, literature as a career still remained his chief ambition. While preparing for his Master's degree, he thought of a novel that should revive the Athens of the fifth century, and to catch the necessary atmosphere, he went to Greece in 1923.

The Acropolis, the Parthenon, in the stupendous Attic light, filled him with enthusiasm. The journey was simply an early breath of light and liberty, only a preliminary tremor : *Hipparete*, a narrative which he wrote on his return, was still full of the influence of Mistral.

That voyage, of itself, did not convert Michel. It was not until 1926 that he broke free. He liberated me, too, including me in his newest discoveries : as far back as my memories go, I find his presence necessary at my side, his thought guiding me.

As we grew up, life failed to separate us. On the contrary, we met it shoulder to shoulder, and if his were the better part, if he ' transformed unceasingly to light and flame all that touched him,' [1] perhaps I helped to make fuller and more effectual our joint efforts.

During his military service in Morocco, he knew a ruder life. He was stirred by the contrasts offered by the ancient Orient, which prompted an essay on

[1] Nietzsche : *The Joyful Science.*

The Humanity of African Towns. At the same time, a friend, Emile Benveniste, introduced him to new masters : Rimbaud, Nietzsche, Walt Whitman. His enthusiasms were fanned also by books such as *les Nourritures terrestres* and *Tête d'Or.*

Then my brother developed a profound scorn for literature, for art for art's sake. And it must be added that family, country, and religion also were suffocating walls around him ; if he accepted them at all, it was with a bad grace. It was so much better to move towards an unknown goal, to try the strength of his opinion, the strength of his body, the violence of his yearnings : ' not to search for the absolute, but only life.'

He wrote :

> *I have every hunger and every thirst.*
> *I stay only with that which enlarges my youth.*
> *Nothing is near to me save all appetite.*
> *I am shaken by all things.*
> *I am heedless.*
> *Everything pleases me, draws me.*
>> *[. . . I long to caress the many breasts of Diana*
>> *of the Ephesians.]*
> *I shall be wallowing in earthly things.*
> *And I LAUGH as though nothing were hidden from me.*
> *I welcome disorder in my spirit as in nature.*
> *I have followed disorder.*
> *I have compelled my spirit to accept it.*
> *I have wrestled with the futile restriction of old ideas,*
> *And in the succession of joy and grief I have found the*
>> *tree of knowledge.*

.   .   .   .

But let me know no mercy to the past, to love only the
    present.
Have no bone to pick—
Not a bone !
And above all not to imitate that saint who turned again
    to his own vomit.

          .   .   .   .

What greater satisfaction, finally, than to scorn
things that once were pleasing : what could be keener
and stronger than to ridicule the past, to discard the
substance of yesterday ?

And, if my brother continued to write, it was to taste
that joy.   In it he found the ' chance to exercise himself,
and to thrive : above all, to develop.'   He wrote ' for
the sake of the effectual study it compelled him to make
of himself ' ; but, writing pleased him also from the
point of view of craftsmanship : it was ' a problem
calling for the co-ordination of hand and intellect.'

He wrote a novel, which he intended to call ' Moving
On ' or ' Son of the Sun,' in which he sought to portray
his hero in search of his own truth, and to plunge him
into a tide that flowed and ebbed, and which should
exalt him or drive him more deeply into materialism
and even into uncleanness.   He purposed ' complete
upheavals, struggles which should overthrow a state
once deemed perfect : the best.'

From 1928 onwards, he wrote scenarios also,
for the films, considering the necessary technique a
splendid medium of expression, and whose conven-
tions he mastered.   His idea was to produce an
unaffected story of heroism and passion, close to life
and stripped to essentials, in the manner of the Russian
school, in which he intended a new use of sound effects.

Craftsman in words and imagery, my brother did not look on with indifference as I took my medical course. On the contrary, we found in that occupation a more perfect balance : while I profited by what he wrote, Michel found real security in knowing that I was a doctor. What either did, he did for both, and the other did not seek to duplicate the experience : it was as though he had already reaped whatever benefit there was to be found. Work or play, we held everything in common, and in common we strove to collect the money which should help us to reach our objectives.

So, in the diversity of our labours and of our pleasures, in their succession and constant flow we came to fulness.

But, whether words, science, love ; there came a time when none of these things was able to satisfy my brother, but left him, instead, burdened by discontent. New ideas haunted him.

He wrote of action :

' When I read that Leonardo da Vinci, before beginning the equestrian statue of Sforza, spent six years studying the anatomy of the horse, my blood is stirred, and I admire Leonardo.

' There you have the evidence of a sublime egotism.

' He turned every conceivable interest, his whole life and being, to the one undertaking. You tell me that during those six years other studies called for attention.

' True enough : say ten, it does not matter : fortifications, drainage, flying machines ! Leonardo had a zest for any interest the world could produce. He made it enlarge his whole life.

' That stands squarely against the idle speculation

which only serves to fret us : contradictions that befog our ideas—a hymn to reality, to effort, to the stuff things are made of—an example of that spirit which refuses to be eaten up by introspection and concerns itself with tackling the problem : line, and its simplification in marble.

' It must be used to offset the ill of an Antonin Artaud, who wrote to Jacques Rivière : " I suffer from a terrible sickness of spirit. My ideas fail at every point, from the simple act of thought to its ultimate presentation in words. Words, the making of phrases, the inward ordering of ideas, the natural reactions of the mind : my intellectual existence is my constant pursuit."

' How that ill wears us out—with which his soul is tainted, covered by mustiness—this unravelling of threads. I am possessed by an insatiable thirst for action.

' I admire Leonardo for that simple, grandiose fervour with which he sought to unify the laws of bronze. And I am afraid that the effort must be willed, sought, and that the mingling of acute intellectuality and realization hides some agony. . . .

' Better than Leonardo, I like Costes, when he removes his boots before taking off, the better to feel his controls. Costes has real will-power.

' I am moved to find such a passion for action . . . the thrill, short or enduring, of one who tackles something with enthusiasm.

' Above all, I lay hold on this example of a poise that is to be envied.

' He does not put his mind on a pedestal. It is his servant, like his hand or foot, helping him only to concentrate, to control the movements of his members, and it is so distributed through him that it is not exactly in his head, but as much in his hands, in his feet, in his eyes. That is what fits him for his work. Fit, first of all, to be a pilot.'

.   .   .   .

The need grew for my brother to find some undertaking difficult enough to exercise his whole being, body and soul.

At another time, he wrote :

' This joy (perhaps demoniacal, Auclair might say) which is in me since I came back from Morocco ! Rising from a feeling of freedom. Sometimes it is as though I were an angel. And sometimes it comes at me too strongly. Joy is no easier to bear than sorrow. I am at a sharp corner.

' If I am to recapture this joy, I must come to the parting of the ways, must enter into some especial danger, and I must treat that danger with contempt. After that I shall breathe again, welcome the joy so new—the same perhaps ; but welcome. Otherwise, I shall suffocate.'

This uneasiness, this anticipation, found their echo in me. Soon, they crept into our conversation, and finally became our obsession. We were constantly on the look-out for anything that might lead us to the new departure, to the desired adventure, drawn by anything that was heroic, mysterious, or fundamentally human.

Very soon, the name *Rio de Oro* began to torment us unceasingly. We came across it in each one of the

adventures, tragic sometimes, of the pilots of the
Aéropostale [1] when they were driven to forced landings

[1] ' It is common knowledge,' wrote General Armengaud, in his
book *Pacification of Unoccupied African Territories* (Paris, Berger
Levrault, 1930), pp. 32 ff., ' that this air-route has one serious
weakness : it must cross the country of independent tribes for
more than 1500 kilometres. For landing-places it must make use
of districts occupied by the Spanish forces ; but from which they
cannot move without the risk of capture : Cap Juba and Villa
Cisneros.

Should the aeroplane be forced down between these two
points, it falls into the hands of the Moors, and the people in it
are carried into captivity. The thick mist often to be found on
the coast frequently makes it impracticable to follow the seaboard,
and the aeroplane must be turned inland, which again increases
the risk of falling among bands of raiders, whose sole occupation
and chief means of livelihood lies in the pillaging of caravans
which pass their way, and in holding them to ransom.

That is what may happen and what, unfortunately, does
happen from time to time.

Reine, the pilot, acting as convoy to Count de La Vaux, vice-
President of the Aéro Club of France, made a forced landing and
was taken prisoner in the western Anti-Atlas, actually in the zone
of French influence. Happily, negotiations for his release soon
had a successful issue, but it might not be the same to-day, the
western Anti-Atlas having become more hostile since that time.

In 1927, Gourp, a pilot, and two passengers, were captured.
One of the passengers was murdered, and Gourp seriously
wounded. He was carried to Casablanca, where he died of his
wounds. The second passenger, a native interpreter, was spared.

Pilot Mermoz, captured in his turn, was ransomed after about
a week. The Odyssey of the Uruguayan airmen, who left France
to cross the Atlantic, and came down on the coasts of Rio de Oro
to be ransomed at considerable cost, has been related at length in
the press.

In 1928 it was the turn of the pilot Vidal, captured in the
French zone, south of Agadir, by the Moors, then of Reine and
Serre. On June 28, for the second time, Reine and the engineer

in that part of the Sahara lying between south Morocco and Mauretania, a land the like of which scarcely exists elsewhere, peopled by Moors who grow increasingly ferocious, steadily more hostile to Europeans, dreading the coming of the time when their lands will be thrown open by force. For the present they hide themselves in their sands, and it goes ill with any one who falls into their hands. If he is not murdered, the best he can anticipate is a miserable captivity.

The adventure began to take a definite shape when we saw, in that part of the map which is left white, one solitary spot, situated at the junction of a number of tracks, and said to be the lair of the Moors of the Atlantic Sahara, their centre of brigandage and fanaticism : Smara.

That spot, which some placed here, some there,[1] became our objective.

Serre, of the Compagnie Générale Aéropostale, came down in the interior of Rio de Oro. During the four months of their captivity they were traded among the various tribes, who bought and sold them like slaves: the terms demanded for their release grew steadily, and at last assumed such proportions — thousands of pesetas, hundreds of camels, guns, &c., that they could not be accepted.

Ultimately, one powerful tribe threatened a thoroughgoing raid on the tribe, which held the prisoners unless they secured in exchange the freedom of certain chieftains held prisoners by the French. Finally, at what price we do not know, these two heroic pioneers of French commercial aviation were set free and restored to their despairing families, and the story of their grim adventure has been published in serial form in a large body of the press.

[1] Slightly west of Long. 12 on the map 1/1,000,000 of the Spanish Sahara and adjacent territories, by Enrique d'Almonte, and more than 40 kilometres to the east on the map 1/2,000,000 (Rio de Oro) of the Army Geographical Service (1927).

My brother studied all previous explorations, referring to books and maps which showed clearly how great the need was for exact information on the region. Speaking generally, it appeared that the location of Smara had remained constant after the explorations of Panet and Camille Douls ; [1] but that, since their time, the nomads had become more aggressive.

So, next door to Morocco, which, already known to Michel, might serve as base, there was a map to

[1] In 1850, Panet, a Senegalese mulatto, travelled from Senegal to the Sous by way of the Atlantic coastal regions. By pretending to be a native Muhammedan, he was able to join a caravan on February 27 ; but, before arriving at the Seguiet el Hamra, he was attacked and robbed by his travelling companions. With the greatest difficulty he succeeded in covering the last half of his journey, and reached Mogador on May 25.

In 1887, Camille Douls, a French explorer, disguised as a Muhammedan, had himself deposited on the shore of the western Sahara, near to Cape Garnet, by fishermen from the Canary Isles. He fell into the hands of a sect of the Ouled Delim. Believed at first to be a Christian, he was robbed, and buried up to the neck in the sand. Having presence of mind enough to repeat passages of the Koran, he was released by his captors, who then took him for a Muhammedan. For five months he was with the tribe on its wanderings. After penetrating deep into the sand-dunes to the east, the tribe moved back again to the Atlantic, near to Cape Bojador, followed the coast, and came to the Seguiet el Hamra. From that point Douls travelled as far as Tindouf and returned to the Atlantic coast.

Douls was affianced to a young Moorish girl, and manœuvred leave to go to Morocco to fetch the dowry. Crossing the Oued Dra in May 1887, he reached Goulimin and then Agadir, visited Marrakech, and finally embarked at Mogador for France. A year later, while trying to reach the Niger from Tafilalet, Douls was murdered by his guides.

correct, a town to investigate, in spite of the hostility
of the tribes and of the desert : the chance of action
and the spice of danger.

The idea gave my brother no rest.   In a few months
he could have completed his novel, have produced the
film, polished up his essays.   He would not take the
time.   The thought of postponing his departure did not
even occur to him.   For a year the project had been
allowed to ripen, and now his decision was irrevocable.

Yet, immediately he entered upon the adventure,
other ideas began to swarm.   After he had proven
himself to himself : after this time of solitude, would
there not be the greater task to undertake—the conviction of others ?

Undoubtedly, but he kept everything in the background to await his return.

If I have mentioned every form of activity that
called us, let nobody believe that our efforts were
spasmodic.   How we should have fought against that !
Certainly, we came at life from all sides, and so found
ourselves constantly renewed, but we treasured the
bond that tied all these things together.   I know of
nothing which better expresses that bond than this
thought of Leonardo da Vinci, which Michel read in
the *Mystère en pleine lumière* by Maurice Barrès, and
which he copied out, to hang in our room where we
could see it :

> *As a day well spent gives a joy to sleep,*
> *So a life well used gives a joy to death.*

* * *

The idea of the expedition goes back to the beginning
of September 1929.   So that we had a year in which to

study it on every side, discover the means of accomplishing our end, and collect the necessary funds.

Having rejected the aeroplane, which could not have given us the intimate knowledge of the country that we wanted, we thought for a while of getting together a large caravan, in which we could pass unnoticed, taking with us an interpreter, a navigator, and a cinematographer, whose services we would engage. Michel would be in full command of the expedition, while I should look after the medical side.

Yet, to leave in such numbers would have invited the unwelcome attention of the French authorities, who would have prevented our going ; besides which, the tribesmen would easily have nosed out the presence of five Europeans in one caravan.

Then we thought of going about it in another way : Michel would go, either alone, or with me.

Exact preparation for the expedition could only be perfected on the spot. We came to no final decision; but, after making certain of assistance should need arise, Michel left for Morocco. The object of his visit was to find one man who, if my brother were able to rouse his interest in our project, could help us with advice, and perhaps in a more practical manner : the caid Haddou.[1]

Should Michel find him unresponsive, he would try to make contact with native traders. He was to keep me informed of every turn of events, and tell me when to join him, either with one or several colleagues or, it might be, alone.

---

[1] Caid Haddou, former minister of Abd el Krim, surrendered his arms to France in 1926. Since that date he has been living, compulsorily, in the neighbourhood of Mogador.

On August 20, as soon as he arrived at Mogador, Michel saw the caid Haddou. Each of the following days was marked by a new conference. Concerning one of them, Michel wrote :

' I felt very strong in myself ; very much on the point of bringing things to pass : very wily. I spoke easily, with enthusiasm—my head thrown forward a little. I remember rubbing my hands together a little—rather moist—which I could scarcely feel (a suggestion of the ease I felt)—with a sort of quiet jubilation.

' I was aware of my attitude : my eyes full of desire and contentment. The thing is suddenly much nearer. The adventure is there : possible. The adventure is going to be made. I can see what it looks like. The puzzle is solved. All the pieces that once perplexed me come together, join up. The useless stuff falls away, disappears.

.   .   .   .   .   .

' Of course I shall not always be like this. Weariness ! Possibly my end may be like Turenne's.[1] There is crest and trough to every wave ; but, when you are in the trough, remember the crest.'

The eagerness with which Michel spoke of his intentions ; the readiness with which he agreed to have the crown of one of his teeth removed, or to be circumcised if it proved advisable ; the scorn he showed for discomfort and the risk of captivity, wounds, or even death, persuaded the caid Haddou to help

[1] Marshal of France, killed by a spent bullet at the height of his fame.

him. He grasped the supreme importance of the raid. He was aware that a group of aviators had flown over Smara a few weeks previously, and anticipated that Michel would not be the only explorer wanting to reach Rio de Oro.

Such news flogged the impatience of my brother. He learned what he could of the state of the dissident tribes from the natives he met with the caid, people who knew south Morocco: Goulimin, the Oued Dra, and, by hearsay, the Seguiet el Hamra, Smara, and the Reguibat.

Obviously, all contact with official circles would have to be avoided, and the organization of a large caravan was out of the question.

Then : were we both to go ? As a doctor, I should undoubtedly have been useful, but it would have been more difficult for two of us to travel in disguise. Besides, a base in the pacified zone was essential. That part I could play better than any one else. So it was decided that Michel should go on alone, and that I should be in readiness to go to the rescue, in case he were wounded or taken captive.

Step by step the plans were laid. He would travel in Berber costume, accompanied by natives, assuming his disguise *en route*, between Agadir and Tiznit. Following that trail, he would come to the dissident tribes. Should he be recognized, Michel would pass himself off as a deserter from the Foreign Legion—English, German, or Danish—trying to reach the Spanish frontier.[1]

The journey would be made quickly : Michel had

---

[1] Actually, El Mahboul had recourse to another stratagem : to the guides and to the inhabitants of Tigilit who knew of his presence, Michel was an American looking for trade with the Moors, especially interested in mines.

always wanted it so : it was an essential factor of success—a dash in two sections : first to the Oued Dra, then beyond the Dra to Smara, across a desert region peopled by the nomad tribes of the Reguibat, Izargiin, &c.

The start would have to be made with the least possible delay, in a week or so, since the visits of Michel to the caid Haddou could not long fail to rouse suspicion in Mogador.

On August 23 he wrote :

' I forget everything : France ! Nothing is wanting. Only one thing interests me now, and that completely : this adventure. I am already in it. It does me good to realize that I am self-controlled, calm. Besides, I must be : how could I undertake such an affair with an uneasy mind ?

' Only Jean's company would increase my happiness. . . ."

* * *

There remained only the task of choosing a man to whom Michel could delegate the practical organization of the raid, and the responsibility of negotiating with the tribes whose territory was crossed on the way. Michel himself was unable to speak their language.[1]

The caid Haddou recommended to Michel one

---

[1] My brother had only learned a few Arabic and Berber words, and the chehada (Muhammedan confession of faith), but he carried in his baggage a text-book by Laoust on Moroccan Berber. It was this latter book which made it possible for him to build up a small French-Berber dictionary during his second stay at Tigilit.

Ahmed ben Hamou el Mahboul,[1] a native of the district of Imgrad (Tamanar group), a trader in tirza wood, with an established connexion in south Morocco. He was intimately acquainted with the tribes as far as Goulimin and the Oued Noun, where he had many friends. In addition to this, on several occasions he had given evidence of his intelligence and loyalty to the caid Haddou.

El Mahboul was at Oran. A letter from the caid told him to join me as I came through, and to follow me to Mogador.

Michel wrote me to that effect, and then waited impatiently for news of my arrival in Africa.

It was during this period that he wrote the following poem :

Smara, town of our illusions . . .

As ravishers we press towards thee,
But also as penitents we come.
And to the friend, or to one who questions us on the way, we
    shall say 'I know you not.'
We travel towards that bourne
Which the dawn floods to overflowing
And purifies.
Sweet water shall be in her streams
And there, drink shall not be denied us.
And the sound of flowing waters shall swell in the silence :

---

[1] Although El Mahboul spoke no French, my brother had scarcely any trouble in talking with him during the raid. I myself was surprised to find that, in the two days I spent with him, although unused to his language sprinkled with its few words of French, I understood almost all that he said. That was because in practice he expressed himself quite as much by gesture as in words, touching his forehead, shoulders, &c., and becoming quite easily understandable.

Bodies and weary hearts shall enter again into gentler days.
Thence we shall go armed,
As they who fear neither contumely nor favour,
Towards the place of the wrestling of men, for the accomplish-
    ment of our labour.

On September 1 I saw El Mahboul in the native
quarter of Oran, and two days later we arrived at
Mogador together.

El Mahboul was given definite instructions, and
suggested that, during the first part of the journey,
as far as the Oued Dra, in a fairly populous district,
where caravans were numerous, Michel should travel
disguised as a woman, which would lessen the risk
of their being discovered. Later, in the region of
Tamanar, he would collect natives to go with Michel :
two women, his brother Larbi, and a certain Ali ou
Boujma, whom El Mahboul called simply Chibani.[1]
This latter had never been to Smara, but could easily
obtain the necessary guides, thanks to his connexions
in the region of the Dra.

On September 8, Michel, El Mahboul, and I had
a last interview with the caid Haddou, and it was
decided that, as far as the Dra, in order to maintain
the appearance of a peaceful little family in course of
migration, no arms should be carried. If the *baroud* [2]
were encountered on the way, they would camp until
such time as the road should be clear.

Once more we went over the means of communica-
tion between Michel and myself. He would send one
or other of his guides to me. For my part, I would

[1] The old fellow.
[2] Hostile raid, by armed tribesmen, on another tribe or
caravan.

make use of the same messengers, or of other *rekkas* [1] to be found by the caid Haddou.

I was not to enter the territory of the independent tribes unless Michel were wounded, or my presence became necessary for some other reason. If he were taken prisoner, Michel would get word through to me, and I would take immediate steps to obtain his ransom.

He took with him two watches, two compasses, two cameras, $6\frac{1}{2}$ by 11 cm., whose operation was explained to El Mahboul, so that he could take photographs of Michel on the journey ; and medicines. I foresaw the possibility of their need in case of wounds and sores, dysentery, malaria, and snake-bite.

It was agreed that Michel should go entirely un-armed, to avoid arousing suspicion in his guides.

El Mahboul estimated the cost of the expedition at about 15,000 francs [2] for the guides, passage-money, and rations.

We arranged a meeting for the Wednesday following, September 10, at about six o'clock in the evening, when Michel would join El Mahboul on the bank of the Oued Massa, about twenty miles north of Tiznit.

I travelled as far as that point with Michel, but by way of Marrakech. A departure from Mogador towards the south could not have been made without attracting unwelcome attention.

At Marrakech we made our last purchases, and

[1] Runners.

[2] But he specified that this sum should be carried in 50- and 100-franc notes of the Bank of Morocco, which, being printed in Arabic characters, were negotiable even among the independent tribes of the interior.

on September 10 Michel and I took our places in the
motor-car which was to take us to the Oued Massa.

The night before, while we talked, Michel broke off,
to write this draft, which he read over to me :

' As they who cry " Take away the chocks ! " '

' For a leap which lifts us out of an obscure and
impersonal existence to bright, enduring definition,
in life and then in death.

.   .   .   .

' The strife of the ego in an act of the will, which
compels a change of nature.

' Like specks of gold in a mass of earth, collected by
the discoverer into a single nugget, appreciable and
refined.

' The Noun passed, and the Dra—stages in the
desired adjustment—then the first touch of the sacred
earth of the town.'

During the long run by motor, we were careful to
avoid inquisitive eyes. Delayed by more than four
hours through the overflow of the Oued Tamri which
cut the road beyond Tamanar, night had fallen before
we went through Agadir.

From that point, a night ride which seemed unending
along a terrible track which sometimes we lost, in
spite of the headlights and a brilliant moon. Once
we sank so deeply into the sand that it was necessary
to dismount and haul the car free.

Finally, making a turn, we descended a slope to the
bridge which crosses the Oued Massa.

El Mahboul and his people were asleep under a
tree lower down. We took our baggage near to them.
Michel got out of his European clothes, and El Mahboul

helped him into the costume of a Berber woman. Then, while Michel stood, anxious as to the correctness of his veils, he allowed the elder of the two women to adjust a knot here, a fold there.

Unobtrusively, El Mahboul took the bundles of 50-franc notes which I passed to him, and stowed them away in his bag. Very quickly he secreted in little canvas bags the things we had brought. Nobody said a word, everything was done in silence. I said a quick ' good-bye ' to my brother, and, picking up the clothes he had just discarded, hurried to the car.

I returned to Marrakech, and a fortnight later was in Mogador again, where the messengers from my brother were to report.

* * *

I am under great obligation to the following people who have helped me in making a fitting presentation of this journal : to M. Paul Hartman, and especially to Professor Louis Massignon and M. Henri Massis.

I should like also to express my gratitude to MM. Raoul Auclair, Emile Benveniste, and Fernand Chapouthier. By advice which they gave freely at all times they became in some measure my collaborators in the publication of my brother's notes : an expression of their loyalty to the memory of their friend.

My thanks are due no less to M. Jean Célérier, director of studies at the Institut des Hautes Études, Rabat ; Captain de La Chapelle and Commandant Robert Montagne, whose counsel helped me to put in order the geographical data ; Lieut.-Colonel Maurice Bernard, for assistance in correlating the itineraries and arranging the map ; M. A. Meunier, geographer to the Ministry for the Colonies, who undertook the verification of the map ; Professor Auguste Chevalier, of the Museum, who identified the specimens of plants brought back by my brother ; M. Théodore Monod, assistant at the Museum ; M. J. Orcel, who examined the rock specimen I submitted to him.

Nor can I forget Professors Augustin Bernard, Alfred Martineau, and Jean Brunhes (the latter unfortunately since deceased), for the way in which they received my brother before he left on his expedition.

Since my return, I have found in Professor Augustin Bernard a support that is inestimable.

THE JOURNAL OF
MICHEL VIEUCHANGE

I

DISGUISED AS A WOMAN

Thursday, September 11.

The start. Heelless slippers. From the outset I found much discomfort, screwing up my toes in vain. The road : *bled* [1] on either side, in the moonlight. We covered two, three miles. I kept as close to the women as I could. We left the track for a sort of ditch in the *bled*, into which we dropped and lay down. I was between El Mahboul and Larbi. Slippers under my head. Fatigue. I was soon asleep.

Awoke about five a.m. We took the track again, like a nice little family on the road. Camel drivers, whose line we crossed. I was uneasy, because my ankles were too white.

Four hours on the road. Very hard going. Sometimes it seemed that I could go no farther. Feet swollen, little patches where the skin had chafed. Then, the pain overcome, it left me a little calmer.

We crossed Ahl Madher, a small hamlet.

I walked. That is my only objective—to keep going. There is no longer day or night for me. One single thing to do : to arrive. I will sleep anywhere, suffer anything.

Tiznit could be seen, a little over a mile away. Scrub palms standing out from a group of houses with

---

[1] Prairie-like open country.

25

flat roofs and walls of earth. Cactus hedges. The *bled* all round, flat and stony.

We left the track, an awful moment ! and crossed little gullies, full of stones. Faint trails, almost parallel, hardly defined, save by stones kicked out of the way in the course of years by the feet of men and beasts. Still, the going was better there.

I thought of Jeannie, of Jean, of Perros. I sang inaudibly " I kiss your little hand, Madame," so that I might forget my feet. But my feet insisted. Then, a phrase of the song awoke sweeter thoughts.

After a time, El Mahboul came to my side and indicated a row of buildings whose walls looked like the earth of the *bled*. A souk,[1] still a long way off. I was afraid to ask them to stop for a while. Luckily, we came to a grove, nearer, surrounded by crumbling low walls of earth. A gap. I went in with El Mahboul and Larbi. El Mahboul talked the whole time we were on the move. Scheming.

In the grove, they made me change my clothes. No longer the red tunic. A large haik, blue, like those of the Dra. I got my miserable feet out of my slippers.

(Immediately, they brought me tea. I could have shouted for joy. I heard the bubbling of the saucepan over a fire between three stones at the foot of a young palm-tree. A few yards away, my guides drank also, exchanging comments and inhaling noisily.

How good it was !

I had forgotten that it was so good to drink.)

In new clothes. They made me go farther into the grove, where I lay down, bare feet on the cool earth.

[1] Market.

Poor feet, how they hurt ! I did not know where to put them so that I should no longer feel them.

El Mahboul made me understand that he was going to Tiznit with Chibani, and that I could sleep while they were gone. I stretched myself out, slippers under my head, and I slept . . . not soundly ; but each time I awoke was conscious of less pain in my feet.

I roused completely. I saw the elder of the women hunting for twigs here and there in the orchard. I heard her blowing her fire. I smelt the marvellous, sumptuous perfume of mint, when Larbi put it into the hood of his burnous to ward off the flies. And I rejoiced greatly. I thought of water, but I knew that soon I should drink. I welcomed my thirst. Larbi took a slice of a sort of pumpkin, cleaned it, cut it into small pieces, I saw also, appetising bits of meat on the twigs.

Then I changed my clothes again, with the help of Larbi. Over my white tunic, a black one. Then I lay down again. Immediately my foot or my hand (too white) became uncovered, Larbi hid them with a rough and rather surly pull at my clothes.

I find that he rather overdoes this covering business : blue haïk, and then thick white haïk. I suffocate, the more because my veil comes almost up to my eyes, above my nose. It seems pretty hard.

Still, when I asked him for writing materials, he obeyed. . . .

El Mahboul and Chibani returned with provisions. They left me in peace, and while I wrote, El Mahboul brought me the first cup of tea, then a second, and the young girl brought me a third. My writing was further interrupted while we ate.

We sat around a sort of stew, in which everybody hunted for his portion with his fingers, Arab fashion : then a drink of water—discoloured water, drawn from the goatskin, with a strong taste of the skin and a sediment of black dust. But it was water. It was good : cool.

Then I withdrew a little farther, to write this.

I shall try to take one or two photographs. But El Mahboul has gone again. Shall I make a bloomer ? We shall see.

Friday, September 12.

(Continuing from where I left off yesterday.)

Lying drowsily beside Larbi, he touched me, and, showing me the half of a pomegranate, peeled off the yellow skin and gave me a handful of the seeds, which I took in the palm of my hand. Lying flat on my face, I ate from my hand, taking the seeds in a single mouthful and chewing them. The juice spurted into my throat.

. . . To the last moment the juice is good, and, at the end the pulp of crushed seeds leaves a pleasant tartness which lasts for a long time. . . .

Impatiently I awaited every move of Larbi, who gave me more seeds. Not one of them was wasted. I eyed them lovingly before putting them into my mouth. They were of a pale rose colour at one end, changing imperceptibly to a translucent white : a colour as fresh as the juice is good.

Larbi cut my finger nails to his liking, with his knife.

Then I rested. I was drowsing when El Mahboul and Chibani came back from the souk with two asses.

While they were getting things together to make a fresh start, I took a few photographs.

We moved on about 3.30 or 4 o'clock.

El Mahboul, without my knowing it, took my slippers to the souk. He had two small pieces added to the sides which grip the heel, so that now I can walk very easily. My feet are still sore ; but, taken altogether, I am not in pain.

I rode one of the donkeys, like a horsewoman, across the panniers. Ahead of me, on the other donkey, rode El Mahboul. Like mine, it also carried a pannier on either side. A water-skin in one of the hampers. The teapot near the rump.

The women always walk. What energy they possess, these Arab women. As soon as we make a halt, it is they who gather the wood, build a fire between three stones . . . and often they have to blow a long time to get it going.

We skirted Tiznit. The plain littered with stones. Larbi and Chibani left us, going alone into Tiznit to buy barley for the beasts, to catch up with us later in open country. We continued across the stony plain.

On the right, Tiznit, with its ramparts and flat roofs, its sea of verdure, and, a little higher, the crowns of the palms.

Enclosing the plain, to the left and ahead : the djebel [1] not very considerable, at least seen from where we were.

We travelled until sunset, Larbi and Chibani not yet having caught up. Tiznit always in sight. Even the seven o'clock prayer of the muezzin was audible,

[1] Mountain (Ighir Mellouln).

followed by a French bugle call—farewell to the West—
then silence. To-morrow, we shall finally lose contact
with the conquered territory.

The sun still shone on the mountains beyond Tiznit :
pale green sky above ; but, to the left, the mountains
and sky were darkening. How the sun caresses the
earth here.

Bored by the slow going, El Mahboul called a halt in
the middle of a vast plain. I took the chance, and
shaved my legs. The shaving-cream worked like a
charm.

El Mahboul left me with the two women and the
asses, and went off to look for Larbi and his companion, but returned without having found them.

Carefully, I stained my legs, arms, and hands with
permanganate of potash, but the solution was too
weak, so the result was not too good.

Fed-up with waiting, El Mahboul decided to move
on without the others.

As we went, I was afraid to ride the donkey. It
grew dark, and the ass stumbled so often ; but I
stumbled myself, wrenching my feet. Still, I did not
suffer as I did this morning . . . and last night.

We kept going for a while. I opened my blue veil
slightly, in the gloom, so that I could breathe. I was
ahead, leading one of the donkeys, when I heard voices
in the rear : Larbi and Chibani, who had overtaken
us.

How could they find us in the dark ?

They argued vociferously with El Mahboul, who
flung his arms about : obviously in a bad humour.
Discussing the missed rendezvous, undoubtedly.

Still we continued. It began to be hard going. I

was just about to get on to the donkey when we stopped
for food. The journey had swollen my feet again and,
stretched on a sack, my feet bare, it was a real delight
to feel the cool air on them. I was absolutely flat on
my back—the magnificent sky above—the cool wind
on my feet (so that I found their pain almost agreeable)
—my face entirely uncovered.

But the pleasure of the moment was utterly spoiled
by the smoke of two fires the women started, and which
was blown into my eyes by the wind. I was forced to
get up : my eyes full of tears, my nose running.

The Arabs breathed the smoke without so much as a
frown.

Dinner. Stew, as usual. I was not very hungry ;
but, how good the mint tea seemed ! El Mahboul
told me it came from Tiznit, the best in Morocco—in
all the world. I took a leaf of mint and crushed it in
my hand. I put one in my nostril. Never have I
breathed so rich, so refreshing a perfume. What is
the mint of France . . . or of anywhere else ?

I understood that we were to go no farther during
the night. Lying near to El Mahboul, Larbi passed
me another djellaba.[1] It was very cold. Everybody
suffered because of it. I heard the women shivering,
their teeth chattering, complaining, when I awoke
in the middle of the night under a brilliant moon.

Larbi was the only one to say his prayers before
going to sleep.

In the middle of the night, we started again. I rode
one of the donkeys, and having hardly had a wink of
sleep the night through was immediately tortured by

[1] Native cloak with hood.

sleepiness. I did not know what to do : stare at
something, or concentrate my mind on a problem.
I fidgeted, and in spite of myself suddenly became
numb, narrowly escaping falling off the ass and making
a sudden lunge to steady myself which threw the ass
to his knees. I should have preferred to walk, to
keep myself awake, and could not understand why
El Mahboul insisted on my riding. Perhaps he wanted
me to save my strength, since I shall have to travel on
foot in the mountains. We may even have to push the
animals.

Our way crossed camel-caravans. I tried to count
them, to keep off sleep.

. . . The shouts of the drivers to recall the animals
when they broke the line. The drivers : thick-set,
bearded little men, with Etruscan heads : dark-blue
tunics slit at the sides, through which their brown
bodies could be seen. Sometimes one of them stopped
his beast, and forced it to lie down at the side of the
track, so that he could adjust the load : camel screams
. . . weird ; the way the animal squats down :
strange position of the hind legs. The camel screaming
throughout the operation.

In the greenery, we saw a large town, very like
Tiznit. Same appearance : Aït Jerra.[1] There the
caid El Ayadi lives in a magnificent stronghold—which
we saw later, having gone the length of the town :
monumental entrance, large courtyard, and collection
of buildings.

We skirted the town at about 200 yards. Very long ;
it appeared to me (I closed my haik so tightly that my

[1] Talaïnt.

view of it was only fragmentary), to follow the rise
and fall of the site. Houses with flat roofs : walls of
reddish earth. Gardens, groves of rich green surrounded by hedges.

We moved on to the djebel, then close at hand.

Halt under an old olive tree. I took some photographs, and cleaned myself up a bit. The women
attended to their cooking. Larbi had a bout of
malaria. He shivered : four quinine powders. Food.
They competed among themselves to see who could
belch the better.

I am writing this during the rest, cooled by a
pleasant wind.

A valley. Here and there, yellowish hills, dotted
with little dark patches (trees? bushes?). On the
plain, old arganier trees, here and there thorn bushes.
Earth yellow and stony. Against the brow of the
nearest mountain ; buildings with broken-down walls.

Saturday, September 13. 7 *a.m.*
We followed the valley.

On the back of an ass. El Mahboul also. Beside
us, Chibani. An argument between them, which
lasted for about an hour. I gathered that Chibani
was uneasy : on the return, would the caid [1] put him
into prison? Sometimes the argument ceased, and
Chibani walked beside my ass. I heard him grumbling.
I pulled up the ass and waited for them, by signs
making them understand that they need not be afraid
of that, because I ' knew somebody.' They laughed

[1] The caid of Tamanar.

when they saw that I had gathered the gist of their argument.

Always the same valley : arganier trees, thorn bushes, hills here and there, occasional plantations, hollow roads between hedges ; but practically deserted. Some farms, also ; but the walls often broken down : red ruins among green cactus.

We followed the valley from half-past two to about five o'clock.

Halt when we reached the end of the valley : a cul-de-sac.

The asses lay down, and with their noses on the ground panted as though they were exhausted. The women, and the men too, were footsore and weary, definitely all in, from walking across the stones in the sun. Although I had travelled most of the way on one of the 'asses, the soles of my feet, just behind the toes, were raw, and I could not walk without pain. My first care was to dress them : wash—talcum powder—massage.

Suddenly, they made me lie down, wrapped in my veils, as though I slept. Footsteps, voices coming near. Conversation between the newcomers and El Mahboul and Chibani. After five minutes' talk, a sort of prayer, an exhortation recited in unison. Then the voices and footsteps moved off. They let me uncover myself, and explained : beggars.

During the evening, I don't know why, we did not eat . . . four glasses of tea . . . I like that better. Talk with El Mahboul, Chibani, and the others. They made me understand that after Smara they would take me to a cavern where a river flows (the

underground course of the Dra, no doubt), and where
it is only possible to move by the light of torches,
stooping, but where there is gold. And, as El Mahboul
said, ' If there is, *mezian, mezian* [1] ; if not, to hell
with it.' [2]

What a tale, this hunting for nuggets along the
bed of the Dra !   It would be almost as good as Smara.

Later, showing me some fortress-farms on the side
of a low hill, they made it clear that we could not stay
there for the night . . . the place was inhabited by
robbers. In the dusk, we loaded the asses and moved
on.

We reached the side of the djebel ; but instead of
continuing to cross it during the night, as I had
expected, Chibani, after agreeing with El Mahboul,
left the path and went round one of the strongholds—
walls and tower, with a superstructure of sharp, pointed
battlements. We waited for him a moment, sitting on
the rocks.

I heard his voice. Immediately they made me
cover my nose again with the white veil, which I had
taken off, and as we travelled along the wall to the gate,
El Mahboul gave me my lesson—' Si Madani,' and
showed me the farm, then bowing slightly, took my
hand and kissed the raised finger.

We entered a large courtyard, encircled by walls
and gloomy buildings. They unloaded the asses in a
corner, and I sat, back to the wall, imitating the
posture of Arab women—knees wide apart, holding the
robes, feet spread and not touching. The two women
sat by my side, then lay down, tired out.

[1] Excellent ! excellent !   [2] *Je m'en fous.*

Night swept from the corners, piling itself up in the courtyard. Slowly, the earthen walls, like Mycenaean ramparts, grew less distinct. Only the summit was increasingly sharply outlined against the sky : a tower with pinnacles, the roof of a building covered with thorns.

After a while, a corner of the country could be seen through the door, but at that moment it was a dark cave.

Sometimes a man crossed in the dark, singing. His outline was scarcely discernible. Some lowing cows returned, passing across the entrance. Voices could be heard, the cry of a child in another part of the farm.

El Mahboul swaggered a bit in his rôle of little caid, as he does at every stage of the journey. Larbi held his feet, massaging them, cracking the toes.

Nobody came, and, realizing that there would be no meal, I stretched myself against the wall. The men lay full length beside the baggage, daggers within reach, and soon I heard them sleeping. The women also were asleep. I only was awake. I turned to the wall, or faced the courtyard ; sleep would not come. There was no breeze between the walls. Was it accounted for by the too-gentle night, or was it because I had had too much tea to drink, I wondered. I was not conscious of any fatigue.

The asses munched their oats noisily, and took a step or two in the courtyard, moving the stones. Above me, the sky became lighter over my unveiled face, and soon the moon, between two battlements of the tower, emerged to look at my beard, which I had not been able to shave.

She rose slowly in the heavens, and her light illumined the side of the courtyard where we lay. Unsuccessfully, I tried to sleep. I remembered that, in Paris, when I was in a similar condition, I used to drink one or two glasses of water, and grow drowsy in perspiration.

Quietly, I reached for my slippers, and hunted for the water-skin. They had stuck a peg into the wall and hung the skin up. I unhooked it, untied the string which sealed the neck, and, holding it above my head, I took a drink, letting some run over my clothes.

Then I lay down again. I thought of the joy we shall have on the return from Smara. With how much greater self-confidence we will refuse the humdrum things ; how much more assured our outlook on life will be.

I went back, to drink a second time. The woman, hearing a stone roll, awakened with a cry, sat up, recognized me, and lay down again. Chibani, who was stretched out near the skin, also awoke.

The night was utterly still, so calm. In the country, all that was to be heard was a distant frog. The asses had finished crunching their oats. The moonlight was brilliant ; but at last I went to sleep.

In the morning, El Mahboul roused me. It was daylight, and quickly, before I was able to veil my face, simply hiding my features with my blue haik, they pushed me into a room whose door opened on to the courtyard . . . where I am writing at this moment.

A room divided into two parts. At the end, a wall which comes only to the middle ; on either side of the wall, two small [partition walls]. The floor of one of them is on a higher level. The part where we are, supported by a round pillar (bricks and earth). Ceiling smoked in places, made of small logs and twisted arganier branches packed close together. The pillar has neither base nor capital. Walls of stone and earth. Floor of beaten earth.

I expected that I should stay here for only a few moments at most. About ten o'clock, seeing that we were still not moving, I asked El Mahboul exactly what we were going to do. I think I understood that we were to stay here until seven o'clock this evening, perhaps till to-morrow morning. The reason : we must not seem to be in a hurry, or else they would be surprised and tell the caid.[1]

Unfortunate occurrence : I was sitting with my face unveiled when the owner of the farm poked his nose into the door. Although the room is dark, in contrast with the courtyard, I was afraid he might have seen my beard ; not so very long, but of three days' growth, just the same. Chibani and El Mahboul seemed not too worried about it.

I worked out our itinerary more exactly with El Mahboul and Chibani. From here to the Oued Dra, going by El Akhsas, four or five days' march, I believe. There we leave Larbi and the two women—perhaps I shall be able to send a word to Jean by him, as well as the exposed films and such notes as I have written. One or two days' rest in the neighbourhood of Goulimin, then we leave : Chibani (who has relations throughout all that district), El Mahboul, myself, and two men—by camel, myself in man's clothing like the other four. If we go steadily on we shall reach

[1] The caid Madani.

Smara in seven days : eight or nine, otherwise. At Smara, as much time as I want. According to Chibani, very few houses outside the kasbahs [1] of Ma el Aïnin and the wealthier tribesmen. Tents (2500 ?) scattered over an area about a mile and a quarter wide. No traders. Poverty. Smara/Guir : seven days. (Guir is on the Dra, I believe.) From there to Tiznit ; seven to ten days.

Odd cooking to-day : in a pan (in which the woman Bous takes water to wash her feet, carefully wiping each toe, then soaking her hands again, then the heel and the sole of her foot), sort of maize-meal, on which oil of arganier was poured from a Shell, or similar, can. The whole kneaded and made into little balls. In the mouth, a sticky dough : heavy, lumpish. I reduced the size of mine steadily . . . and I ate some chocolate.

My companions :
Larbi : a naïve sort of fellow, who says his prayers regularly, holds his string of beads, walks ahead when we move ; not particularly jovial.

Bous, the woman : soon used to seeing me, to putting on my haik : abrupt, good worker, merry ; a chatterbox.

Fatima, or more usually Fatma : good stout girl, timid, ignorant (takes my camera for a weapon), does not talk much, afraid to touch me, to look at me.

Chibani : an old fox, untiring, tanned, wrinkled, almost black, gnarled, big nose ; his turban perched comically on his head : gay, agile.

El Mahboul : a sort of Figaro, or rather an Arabian

[1] Citadel.

Giles—I'll find whom he resembles—cheery, chatterbox, likes to be waited on, swaggers ; always plaguing
the girl, but as cunning as they make 'em : explains
himself by signs (description of the donkey, &c.),
sometimes really comic.

Everybody, except perhaps Fatma, delighted to
travel, to disguise me—as pleased as children to shave
me, to look at things, and release the shutter of the
camera.

Sunday, September 14.

(El Akhsas, in the kingdom of the fierce caid Madani.
On a peak. In the valley, a little below, a market
to which Chibani has gone. It is not healthy for a
Frenchman here. What is a little worse is that we are
encamped in such a fashion as to be open to view.
I had to insist in order to get my note-book. And
El Mahboul, up to now, has not been agreeable to
my taking photographs. I shall try again later. I
am swathed in my blue veil as I write.)

Yesterday. All day and all night in that house.
El Mahboul took the opportunity and shaved me. Up
to then I had simply kept my hair hidden. I was free
in the little room. El Mahboul and the others, at a
loose end, looked through our packets, and, opening
them, asked me for explanations. It was really odd
to see me going backwards and forwards, or sitting
down with the Berber manual, or some other com-
promising article in my hand. We could hear the
voices of the owner, or his children, and people walking
overhead. But, in feminine attire I felt reasonably
confident, even out of doors ; free, out of danger,

IN A COURTYARD AT EL BORDJ AÏT SKIRI
MICHEL VIEUCHANGE HAS TAKEN OFF HIS VEIL. SEPTEMBER 19

MICHEL VIEUCHANGE AS A BERBER WOMAN
FROM LEFT TO RIGHT : CHIBANI, BOUS, FATMA OUTANA, LARBI.
PHOTOGRAPH TAKEN BY EL MAHBOUL. SEPTEMBER 11

although I was anxious to be crossing the Sahara, on the back of a camel, with my face uncovered, head and chest bare.

. . . Under my wraps it is possible to hide pencil and note-book, to make one's toilet. Their folds serve as a handkerchief, they protect from cold and heat, make a sort of cushion. . . .

Dinner in the gloomy courtyard, between sunset and moonrise. Chibani unearthed from some place or other a little lamp with four spouts, an antique. Another thick porridge, heavily peppered, soaked in arganier oil. After two dabs, I could eat no more.

Slept in that garret ; or rather, hardly slept at all. I don't know why sleep escapes me. I spent an hour dressing my right foot by the light of the moon. I was afraid that it would not stand up to the job, but it seems all right now.

Roused at about five o'clock. We left the court-yard and began to tackle the mountain. Just light enough to find a foothold. Rough path. We pushed the asses when it was necessary for them to scale the rocks. The sides of the mountains strewn everywhere with squat, gnarled arganiers . . . red earth and piles of grey stones . . . arganiers and an oily plant shaped like a ball, emerald green : examined closely, a compact sheaf of [pillars] in the form of a phallus.

El Mahboul hammered one of the balls with a stone, to show me the milky fluid which oozed out, and indicated his eyes, doubtless to say that it is blinding or harmful : I don't know. All this, incidentally, in the dawn. No sun, just a brightening of the sky. Ahead

of us, dusk and silence. We could hear cries of ' Oh !
oh ! '—camel-drivers forming their caravan.

When the sun was almost risen, we could see them
about a quarter of a mile away, busy with their beasts,
making them kneel for loading, leading them across
the rocks. Magnificent sight. Stumpy, blue little
men like imps. The beasts—of which, sometimes,
only a long grey neck behind a grey rock could be
seen—wandered in every direction, moving on, or
coming to a halt, standing or lying down. At last, by
degrees, they began their journey in single file.

Spectacle belonging to a country other than my
own, to a different age.

Behind us, the valley. I saw the house (near others)
where we stayed, with ruddy walls, like the soil.
Detached, at the blind end of the valley, was a marabout,[1] very white.

We followed the caravan at some distance. El
Mahboul found a way of borrowing a horse from one
of the caravanners, and made the journey in the saddle
at his ease, proud as a peacock.

We met one or two groups of women, who talked
with Larbi and Bous.

(Concerning that horse : it appears that the gallant
caravanner had originally suggested his animal for
me.)

During these conversations, I kept myself veiled
bezef [2] and made no move.

In about two hours we made the top of the first
peak [3] and began to descend to the valley. Nearing a
souk we left the caravan and gained a height too much
in view for my liking. Mint tea, and more porridge

---

[1] Tomb of a saint.   [2] Very much.   [3] Djebel Sidi Iddir.

with arganier oil. Frightful water, earthy and foul-smelling. I made myself a cup of chocolate, which I found delightful, soaking in it some pieces of barley bread.

It ought to be about midday.

Monday, September 15. 3.15.
Valley of the Oued Noun.

Yesterday, we stayed till about five o'clock camped on that rise from which we saw El Akhsas. Arabs as thick as ants if you looked closely at the valley or the sides of the nearby hills. Chibani, El Mahboul, kept me completely covered. Occasionally the Arabs came to exchange a few words with them. I was uncomfortable. Forced to stay lying down, I hardly knew how to find a comfortable position. Besides, I must always remember to observe certain rules : to lie curled up like a dog, never on the back—to lie on the back indicates the Jewess. In the same way, when I sit : knees never close together, but wide-spread—feet as well. Riding the ass : heels lower than the toes, &c. &c.

I was very anxious to take a photograph of El Akhsas, probably never photographed before. I made a first effort ; but, once up, and having the three men around me, they suddenly became afraid and forced me to sit again. ' *Bezef, bezef* [1] Arabs,' they kept on saying. So I sat down again and waited for half an hour. Then I fixed two pins so that my blue veil would not move, and I could operate beneath it without being seen. Even though that hardly pleased El Mahboul, I moved nearer to the edge of the plateau ; but there,

[1] Much, many.

for the second time, Larbi and El Mahboul pressed so
much against me, jostling me, that the shutter worked
before I was ready. It was the last on the spool, so
there was no remedy.

Chibani (who went to the market) brought back
meat and provisions of all sorts. They made me taste
some grilled liver, which was quite fair. (They wanted
me to eat more ; but I could not, not being hungry.)

At five o'clock we camped at some distance from the
caravanners, some of whom belonged to the same
tribe as Chibani. At nightfall, he called them over,
and, lying on the earth in the shade (at some little
distance from the three women—Bous, Fatma, and
myself), sipped tea with them, Larbi, and El Mahboul.

Bad night. El Mahboul did himself well : bag of
barley under his head, his brother's djellaba to keep out
the cold. For me ; just a bag. And I was not in the
best of humours as it was : I took a considerable risk
trying to get that photograph, and I misfired. I should
have been so glad to get it.

At four o'clock, at the same time as the caravanners,
we made a start.

A long stage . . . the longest, I believe, that we have
done : from four o'clock [in the morning] to nearly
two o'clock [in the afternoon], which made it possible
to cross a group of mountains [1] and reach the valley
of the Oued Noun. To realize that I was treading
this valley restored my spirits.

. . . Hard moments when we were crossing the
mountain, sometimes on foot, sometimes on the ass ;
but my feet stood up to the journey. Half a dozen

[1] Djebel Aït bou Foul.

times the asses came to grief, with a risk of breaking
our ankles, or pitching us head-over-heels down a
slope. Sometimes I could walk no more. (El
Mahboul rode the burros probably more than I
did.) . . .

We followed the bed of the oued, enclosed by high
banks : valleys where the heat was insufferable, or
valleys that were cool and fresh (the ones with the
steepest banks, which the sun had not yet burned up,
or those open to the wind—how agreeable they were).
Practically no vegetation. Fallen rocks . . . and
more fallen rocks.

. . . It is most interesting, and at the same time
most annoying to follow this camel-caravan. I am
compelled to travel completely veiled. How I want
to have my face free, to walk in freedom. I have to
keep telling myself that this adventure must of necessity
be difficult . . . then I can bear anything.

There is a youngster, the only one in the caravan,
who tags along behind. How agreeable I find him
when he leads the camels, whips them up, intoning
the same songs as the old drivers in his little voice. It
seems to me that, after the *oh ! oh ! oh !*, which continue until a straying camel has returned to the proper
trail, the drivers have another simple call which says,
I suppose, that everything is in order again. The
youngster calls his *oh ! oh ! oh !*, and his other phrases,
and that makes him very attractive. But, little by
little, indiscretion has got the better of him. He turns
back and stares at me, forcing me to keep a careful
watch on all my actions and on my veil, so that my
hands and ankles may be kept out of sight as much as
possible. . . .

With what impatience I watched an opening in the mountains : but always I saw peak beyond peak. Sometimes the crests seemed to be not so high, and I lived in the hope of a valley. Many times I was deceived in that way.

But, at last, after one final spur, our eyes beheld the wide valley of the Oued Noun. As we came down, the cool wind whipped my face. The caravan had gone a little ahead of us, and I walked less hermetically veiled.

The Oued Noun ! How glad I was . . . how glad I am . . . A landmark at last ! A name that I have uttered so many times.

In the valley ; everything flat and without vegetation : a little verdure, and a small town, not so big as Tiznit, surrounded by ramparts, and without relief—it was almost necessary to hunt for it in the plain. El Mahboul said it was Bou Izakarn. I took a photograph of it ; but, unfortunately, the sun was badly placed. Then we continued the descent and reached the valley.

Long, long crossing : a mile or a mile and a half without any shade. Midday sun. Half-way, without stopping the asses, El Mahboul unhooked the water-skin and, holding it above my head, gave me the first drink. Mouth glued to the opening, to the hairy skin, the water spurted down my throat in a stream, and flowed the length of my arms. I no longer noticed the earth or the foul taste of the water. It was cool, it was good. The women drank after me.

We camped finally, near to scraggy bushes and a small arganier tree—a dry branch of the oued, probably : fine sand and gravel. Wherever there was a little shade it was splendid, very cool, because a wind which could be heard overhead when one lay down, which blew through the clothes, made for comfort.

Unable to think of meat without disgust, I prepared my meal in my own fashion : chocolate, sugar, flour, water—a cake like those we eat at home. That did me a world of good. With it, mint tea.

I feel very fit. We are camping here for the night.

The camel-drivers, who are travelling our way, have rifles (Lebels) and bayonets. I was able to read the number on one of them, but cannot recall it.

Chibani and Larbi left us at four o'clock in the morning, returning to El Akhsas to buy a camel.

An Arab, seeing my white ankles, would say to El Mahboul, 'That isn't a woman you are taking along there, it is a man.' El Mahboul does not seem too troubled about it, so I do not worry.

Tuesday, September 16.

Camped in the valley of the Oued Noun for twenty-four hours, always curled up like a dog on the ground, or sitting like an Arab woman. How I should have liked to stretch myself out !

Until about seven o'clock we stayed in the dry bed of the oued. I expected to stay there to sleep, free from observation, the fine sand hollowed to the shape of my body ; to sleep with my legs at full length, my face to the sky. Impatiently I waited for the darkness, because during the day I must retain my veils, keep a

guard over my movements and posture, be on the
watch for the youngster who prowls about. But, out
of the darkness came a shout : the leader of the
caravan, camped about two hundred yards away,
inviting El Mahboul to come nearer for the night.
And immediately El Mahboul rose and busied himself,
loading the asses, packing off, and making us follow
him close to the caravan—prone camels, a line of
silhouettes in the dark, a few small fires, loads piled
up near the beasts. We settled ourselves down twenty
yards away. It was dark, and the moon not yet risen ;
nevertheless, El Mahboul insisted on my lying motion-
less, like a dog, with only the ground beneath me. I
found it impossible to tolerate the hard bed for hours
without moving.

Chibani and Larbi returned with provisions and
perhaps a camel. Their voices in the darkness.
They sat, lit a fire, made tea. In the firelight it was
still more imperative for me not to move. My pelvic
bones hurt, and as El Mahboul was close to me, I took
his hand and made him feel the unprotected bones.
He understood and passed me a sack. That made
me almost comfortable, made sleep more possible.
Chibani's friend came to take tea with him, Larbi
and El Mahboul. Then our fire died down. From
the caravan came the sound of monotonous chants,
very primitive, which also, in their turn, died down.
I slept.

Awakened by the cold, I opened my eyes. A moon,
veiled in fog. Fine drizzle falling. I was frozen
and drenched. I turned over, to warm the colder
side if I could.

Until morning the wet fog dripped and dripped.

At dawn, Chibani led me, with the two women, to a little hollow, where he made a fire to dry our clothes.

I believed that we should start immediately afterwards. Not at all ! It is already two o'clock, and we are still in the little hollow, where at this moment I am stifling under my veils.

At first I put it down to the fog, thinking that they dare not let the camels try the mountain passes for fear that they would slip ; but El Mahboul has just explained that the tribes through whose country we are to travel are anything but peaceful, and that we shall continue with Chibani's friends.

It is impossible for me to say how difficult I find it to keep up this everlasting pretence. The heat, the fatigue, would be nothing ; but, this unending restraint ! It drives me into an absolute frenzy of rage. I have to remind myself that what I am doing is bound to be difficult : that alone calms me down. But I can hardly see the sunset, or where I am—not at all the men who come and go, except by some wearisome subterfuge. Everything annoys me : the women who giggle like idiots because I am irritated by these cloaks, beneath which I blow like a walrus. They begin to be familiar, covering me more than the occasion demands, and simply from an urge to tease, to be a nuisance—otherwise they are the best girls in the world. Bous, yesterday, fell off one of the burros on to the rocks ; a hefty bump. She bruised her arm, and has been rubbing it ever since, muttering her grumbles, and at the same time she regards me with a questioning eye : perhaps she blames me for her tumble.

5 o'clock.

We left the place of which I spoke at two o'clock.
Did two miles, as far as Tagant, a small hamlet similar
to Bou Izakarn. Standing in the middle of the plain :
red ramparts, verdure. It might be described as
similar to the country near the Nile.

But how slow ! We are to wait here until other
caravans arrive, so that we may cross the doubtful
country ahead in some strength.

Wednesday, September 17. Fask.

The delay was not unduly prolonged, since we were
on the march this morning between four and five
o'clock.

Passed yesterday evening lying down, or sitting with
my back to the village, to avoid being seen by the
caravanners encamped by the wall, should I uncover
my face. For safety's sake, I arranged it so that the
opening of my blue veil could only be seen from a part
of the *bled*, covered with stones or bushes, that I could
scan at a glance.

Hardly any dinner . . . and we lay down to sleep
as soon as the sun was set. The early part of the night,
when there was a certain coolness, was very agreeable.
I let my bare feet slip out from underneath my robes.

In the mountain, perhaps a mile or so away from
where we were, stands a famous marabout—which,
naturally, we could not see. But the silence was so
complete that there came to us the voices of men
chanting, or intoning their holy invocations. They
were almost like the songs of Christians, and what an
effect it had, this gravity, this assured faith, untroubled
by doubt, which holds the men of this country in a

serenity comparable to that of the country people of France : not curious about things that are to come. A dangerous fanaticism, perhaps.

It brought home to me how far removed from it all I was—an unsuspected ear listening to hymns that the faithful believed were heard by true-believers only. The hymn focused all my estrangement, all my separation, all my intrusion into a country sure of itself : free. It was as though I violated a secret, heard a forbidden thing. Perhaps that is why I appreciated it so much, found it so full of charm and mystery. So the night, the darkness, became pregnant with the unknown as I kept my vigil : the only alien, the only one able to listen as I did to a sort of revelation ; a hidden mystery, something stolen ; a simple hymn in the night.

The night itself was so cold, so humid, that I did not even close my eyes (each in turn kept watch on account of prowlers ; but in the neighbouring camps, not in ours) ; so cold that I fumed with rage against El Mahboul, who kept his good djellaba to himself ; so cold that I thought of a soft bed, with a beloved body beside me, in place of those women, who pressed close to me in a way so coarse and unpleasant . . . filling me with a certain disgust.

Daylight at last, but a sunless day, misty, which emerged slowly, so slowly from the night, taking hours ; colder perhaps than the night itself ; but more welcome just the same, because it was the forerunner of the sun.

Until the last moment I was uncertain as to what we were going to do. What annoyed me even more was the thought that possibly they did not know themselves.

The joy of climbing on to the donkey—sign that we were on the march.

We were on the plain—a little bundle, a pearl in the short rosary of the caravan. Ahead of us, another little bundle of eight camels, three men, two children. The men had rifles, slung by their straps or balanced horizontally on their shoulders.

After crossing the plain, we entered a range of mountains where there were no trees—a few bushes only, between the rocks. Of prowlers, we saw none whatever.

The donkey, which I rode for about five hours, chafed my bottom in good fashion—preparation for the camel. Always closely veiled, because of the people round us. The sun did not rise until very late.

We found the valley of the Oued Noun again, and travelled for a short distance along a narrow stream of running water whose banks were hidden under clumps of oleanders.

In the plain, which must be compared to a valley of the Loire, but fifty or a hundred times as big—sand ; small bushes—a mass of thick verdure which rose abruptly out of the sand, partly surrounded by red walls. Fask.

We pressed on across the plain, flanking the town at some distance, and went farther on, where we halted in the open country ; but within sight of the town, under a one o'clock sun, I imagine, without so much as a bush for shade.

Not having slept a wink, I lay down, and was instantly asleep.

How long after, I do not know—perhaps an hour—

one of the women roused me to offer me a piece of meat. Luckily it was grilled.

I seemed unwell, my head was heavy. I imagined sunstroke. Then I asked for water, drank some, and poured the rest over my head, or rather over my veils. Soon, by reason of the evaporation, my whole head was quite cool. That seemed good to me ; but the fools of women giggled to see me do it—that is about all they do, and the older of them likes to press herself against me a bit too much.

I was under the impression that we should make a new start this evening, or to-morrow morning at the latest ; but according to what El Mahboul just tells me, it is not at all certain, since there is still the baroud in the neighbourhood.

6.30.

We made a start at about half-past three.

We walked until about half-past five, always following the valley of the Oued Noun ; I understood but am not sure that my understanding was correct, that we must make a detour to avoid the thieves of the main roads.

To-morrow we sleep at the house of the man who owns the horse (the leader of the little caravan with which we are travelling), and, the day after, at the house of one of Chibani's friends. From there, we leave for Smara.

Just before we reached our present position, the plain broadened (I think that at that point we left the valley of the Oued Noun and entered the *bled* called Arouel), the bordering hills seemed to grow smaller—hills quite bare, which the five o'clock sun tinged

with purple. In the plain, every little shrub threw
its shade. At the end of the broadened valley, and
slowly decreasing in height, mountains to the horizon :
ranges resting upon each other in the slanting light.
The plain itself where we are is covered with green
shrubs.

In a little nook, where, although we are alongside the
caravanners, we are safe from prying eyes, I am writing
this. Above my head, some camels browse off a shrub.

Thursday, September 18.

To pass the night in this plain . . . answering a
call from the leader of the caravan, we left our little
redoubt of bushes, and, groping for our baggage,
settled ourselves near to the camels (for fear of the
baroud, no doubt).

I lay beside El Mahboul, who was considerate
enough to cover me with the half of his good woollen
djellaba. Under my head, a mat which is usually
placed on the back of the asses, so that the chafing of
the two panniers will not cause sores. So protected,
I was not cold and was able to sleep. Before I went to
sleep, El Mahboul warned me that, if fighting broke
out, we should go on alone : Chibani, El Mahboul,
and I, mounted on the camel (and doubtless a horse
which the leader of the caravan would lend us). That
was the reason Chibani had taken care to buy the
camel well before reaching the Dra. These fellows
are cunning old foxes.

Always these foggy, dull, drizzly dawns, which last
till about ten o'clock.

Until ten o'clock they let the camels graze, who
wandered here and there among the bushes, nibbling

the leaves covered with little drops of moisture. Then, the operation lasting anything up to an hour, the loading began, during the whole time of which the camels let out their awful screams. Chibani and Larbi worked like the devil, helping the caravanners.

' Good morning ' is said somewhat after this fashion (minor observation in the vein of Herodotus) :
    ' All right ? '
    ' All right ! '
    ' You are all right ? '
    ' Yes, all right ! '
    ' Really all right ? '
    ' Really all right ! '
    ' Sure you're all right ? '
    ' Sure : all right ! '
    ' Then you're all right ? '
    ' Yes, all right ! '
and so on, for some minutes.

About half-past ten, started again across the plain, bordered by the same low, weathered mountains, lying, I think, north-north-east and south-south-west (but I am not positive, the handling of the compass was a little difficult—the same for our direction, which was south-south-west).

A long stage, continuing until five o'clock, without a stop. Always, to the left, at about half a mile, or perhaps three-quarters, hills behind which the Dra flows. So that we are actually in the region of the Dra, parallel to which we marched. Sandy plain—gazelle droppings. Cloudy weather, slightly less so at about four o'clock.

A dreary journey, at varying distances from the little group of camels. Sometimes the load of one or other of the beasts would shift (the load : a huge sack made of striped material, placed on the back and hanging down on either side). Then two camel-drivers would throw themselves at it, taking a stand under the sack on either side, and by jerks get the sack into position again. During the whole time the camel screamed. Tail turned up, hind-pads wide-spread from the knees down—ludicrous.

About five o'clock, a hamlet came into view [El Bordj Aït Skiri], in which was the house of the leader of the caravan, and where he offered us hospitality for the night—backing up to a chain of mountains [1] lying (to the eye) west (north), and east (and a little south).

Ignoring the protests of El Mahboul, I took two photographs, but from such a distance that I am afraid they will show nothing. In any event, they would be useless, taken from a distance. But, coming nearer, I saw a type of village such as few (perhaps no) European eyes can have seen.

No ramparts, but enormous square houses with flat roofs, walls buttressed here and there. Arranged without plan ; but making courtyards, where motion-less men stood in their blue vestments, silver daggers at their side ; a few women ; a white dog.

The walls of some half-ruined houses still remained standing in the courtyards, among houses that were still whole. One would liken them, so far as I could see, to the ruins of an ancient Carthaginian or Mycenaean city.

[1] Djebel Mechbouk(?).

Part of the grandeur of the scenery ; immediately behind the village, rose the bare flank of the mountain, dominating the arid *bled*. Among the houses, that were the same colour as the earth ; not a tree, not a green twig. The courtyards open to the *bled*—houses the same height—one or two square towers—that is all.

We filed past the courtyards as one would in photographing it with a motion-picture camera. I looked on, through an opening in my veil. The people did not stir. We went into one of the courtyards, then into the courtyard of a house where I dismounted. We went under a low door, crossing a bare, dark room . . . sort of stable . . . which led to another narrow court. Our host was with us, and showed us a staircase without handrail, narrow, leading to a small, square room (where I am), absolutely bare, except for a mat on the floor. For ceiling : branches packed close together.

I made my exit by a very low door—less than two feet—and took three photographs.

Here, I have been able to take off my veils, recharge the cameras, look after my feet—which they needed.

It is dark : almost night.

Friday, September 19. 8 *o'clock.*
[*El Bordj Aït Skiri.*]

Slept well, sheltered from the cold.

I believe I am to understand that we stay here until noon. We shall sleep in the *bled*, and to-morrow, towards midday, expect to reach the house of Chibani's nephew.

5 p.m.

We shall not leave until seven p.m., travel until about ten o'clock, sleep in the *bled*, and reach Chibani's nephew about noon to-morrow, it seems.

To-day, I have slept and, taking advantage of the isolation of the little courtyard, have let the sun get at my body. I had not been out of my clothes since we left Tiznit. I have also attended to my feet, &c. My arms and legs were still too pale : I have stained them with permanganate of potash. . . . I have also rubbed my nose and cheeks a little : result, not too bad.

Began to write to Jean.

We are not going ! ! We sleep here. Impossible to get a clear understanding why. We shall start, so it is said, at 3 a.m. How they disgust me, these continual postponements, these too-frequent alterations of my time-table ! And, instead of giving me a clear statement in a word or two, El Mahboul talked and talked. I ended by regarding it as a piece of strategy.

Saturday, September 20.

Yesterday ; the sequel to my friction with El Mahboul : while I was writing, he lay down and shifted the candle so that I could not see. From time to time I asked him for water. His reply : ' There is none.' I said nothing, but when I heard Larbi in the courtyard, getting ready for sleep, I called and he came.

' *Gibb shwia elma*,' [1] I said.

He fetched me a glass of water.

----

[1] Give me a little water.

El Mahboul, leaning on his elbow, blackguarded him, but he took the hint, and roused the women at once to make tea and find the bannocks of barley bread. I looked on, then, tapping him on the shoulder, said :

'El Mahboul, you said to me, " *Oualou elma*," [1] but there was some.'

Then I read him a long lecture in French, which, of course, he could not understand. But I have noticed that to say something they cannot understand always makes a profound impression.

We began to move at ten o'clock. Climbed down to the courtyard by the winding staircase with its enormous steps. In the courtyard the asses and camel were already loaded. Chibani, with a rifle on his shoulder, joined a man near the wall, and talked for a long time in a low voice. Two other armed men appeared and we moved off quickly.

At first : sand, which filtered into my slippers ; but easy going. The only annoyance : the women who would tag along after me, to prevent my getting too far away.

An hour's walk, perhaps. Then the first spurs of the mountain. Bare ankles among the rocks ; sharp stones ; thorn bushes which were not noticeable till too late. I stumbled and cut myself. It was really killing. No sooner was one hurt overcome than the foot twisted or the ankle took a knock.

El Mahboul, of course, dodged it, perched on the camel. That disgusted me. I could have no respect for a man who avoided anything that looked like work.

[1] There is no water.

We continued until two o'clock, and then slept till four. For myself, I could not sleep. I was too cold : my clothes were wringing wet with sweat and fog, soon absolutely frozen. I was shattered with ague. El Mahboul condescended, after about an hour, to offer me a tiny fold of his woollen djellaba. So damp that I had a sort of spasm of rheumatism : impossible to bend my fingers, they were so swollen (incidentally, for two days I have not been able to take off the four rings that I have worn since we left Tiznit).

Happily we started again. I rode one of the asses and waited eagerly for sunrise. That happened suddenly, in a sort of flux, like a golden wave which spread over the face of the earth, leaving small islands of shadow here and there in the little hollows. Then the wave rose, and soon warmed me ; not so quickly as I should have liked though, because of the evaporation from my wet clothes.

We left the mountains, travelling across country that was slightly irregular, but level : beds of small, broken stones, gravel, winding round the small rises. On our left, bare mountains of some size, surmounted by one whose rangy black summit stood out in the sky. I asked Chibani what it was called.

' Tabaïout,' he replied.

About half-past nine we came to a halt for a while among somewhat more plentiful vegetation ; high shrubs. (I am writing at this spot.)

I I

TIGILIT

Sunday, September 21. *Tigilit* [1] (*Aït Bouhou*).

I wonder what I should have said if, instead of
writing to-day when I am rested (although bruised
black and blue), I had told my story at nine or ten
o'clock last night, when, my feet in ribbons, parched,
all in, I could not have moved another inch.

I went through something then : from ten o'clock
on Friday night to nine o'clock on Saturday night—a
twenty-three hours' march on practically an empty
stomach. But could anybody have foreseen such a
stretch : especially the last three or four miles ? We
covered anything from forty to fifty miles. . . . I do
not know exactly.

We resumed the march at about a quarter-past ten.
Mountains all the way, on either side of the valley. A
second peak, on the left, showed its jagged black summit
above the yellowish brows of the others, nearer and
not very high. Again I asked the name : ' Taoulegt.'

Our march—three hired bodyguards either leading
the way, or bringing up the rear. Nobody travels
here without expecting some sudden attack. That
seems incredible in such a barren country, where
there is no sign of habitation. I had to force myself

---

[1] Pronounced with a hard ' g.'

to believe it : the idea would not otherwise have occurred to me.

Halted about the middle of the afternoon among fairly high bushes [Tamaleht]. The men pushed on a little with the three warriors. I stayed stretched out near the two women. Thirst. Larbi brought the teapot full of water and poured some into the lid for me. It was clear, but when I moistened my lips it tasted like a purgative—sulphate of soda. Still, I drank a little.

Again under way. The asses themselves were spent : useless to dream of riding them. El Mahboul paraded on the camel. The three guards took the waterskin to look for better water, and were a long time away. Uneasiness. Chibani stopped in his tracks. I asked El Mahboul ' the *baroud* ? ' Carried off, perhaps. I noticed they went in strength. Then, when our waiting stretched out, without their returning, I began to believe that perhaps they were right to do so. Finally, seeing them in the distance, we moved on.

The country changed. Rocks ; gorges. Rough. Sombre mountains. We passed among them. Soon, at our feet, a deep ravine whose sides were almost perpendicular. However, we went into the gorges [Almerkt], and had to bolster up the camel and the asses, which took fright from time to time, turning back, sniffling and bellowing. Only the stick persuaded them to keep going downhill.

We reached the bottom ; stony bed, and I found what they were seeking : among reeds, a lake, whose sloping edges were made of flat, worn rocks.

Flat on my face, I drank ; drank of water that

tasted of mud, a little stale at that. There could be only very little sun in such a place, because of the narrowness of the gorge. It was cool, and, as the day closed, not very light, compared with the higher reaches.

I kicked off my slippers, and could not resist the urge to soak my aching feet for a moment. The others stayed for a few minutes, paddling. When I lay down to drink, my veil, or rather my veils, slipped, leaving me bare-headed, my hair tousled. Suddenly the women nudged me violently with their elbows. '*Argaz!*' (a man). Without turning, I replaced my blue veil over my hair. Chibani, El Mahboul, Larbi, and the women buzzed like flies that had been scared.

It was easy to gather the cause of their uneasiness, to understand their thoughts as they moved around. The unexpected arrival of a man in such a place is an event. The question always is : 'Is he followed by others ? Is it an ambush ? '

So people must have travelled in France in the seventh century, or in the first century B.C. Always in this overhanging fear.

Every moment they found a new hiding-place for the money : from the camel to the ass, from the ass to the head of one of the women, from the head of the woman to the hood of a burnous. Then we split into two groups—and came together again. Or, we went each his own way. Scheming always, always . . . and one knows that it is their natural habit. That is the state in which they live.

El Mahboul and the newcomer—who looked like a young man to me, with an open face—climbed the banks, pulling the camel. Larbi, the two women, and I took another route. We regained the sun.

Country black and tortured. We walked, and walked. It was almost as dark as night. The sun had set at the end of the narrow, high-banked valley we were following, leaving a sort of orange fog between the dark hills.

Chibani, of whom I had lost sight, . . .

(I understand from El Mahboul that one of the three men who acted as our escort was killed this morning on leaving Tigilit, but I could not quite make out the details : a bullet in the stomach—died immediately.)

. . . reappeared and made us leave the path, already difficult enough, and made us descend in the dark the banks of a sheer and deep ravine [Asder]. We could see there a little ; but I could not think, without fear, that, once we were down, and it became imperative to climb the other side, we should have our fill of danger.

From that moment, to the time when we reached the house where I am now, we had a frightful march, which lasted for about an hour and a half, where once or twice I thought I had broken my ankles, taking short jumps in the dark ; the soles of my feet, heels, toes, unable to bear the slightest touch . . . and still we had to go on, at the risk of cracking our heads below. (The memory of those dark gorges, and of my feet stumbling among the rocks, is likely to wake me with a start often enough in the future.)

. . . At the bottom of the ravine, which we followed among the rocks : feet and ankles trapped between two rocks more than once. . . .

. . . The other bank. A climb which lasted perhaps twenty minutes : terrible ! El Mahboul was a good fellow. He took my hand and helped me along.

Done in ! How I suffered. I wanted to be sick. On which saint to call, I did not know ; or what to do, to keep going. The dark caverns below grew deeper ; but above, if I raised my head, it seemed that the side of the ravine grew higher and higher. However, anger gave me a little relief : anger with Chibani. Why had he made me do all that ? I might have broken my head, or an ankle, and then *makach* [1] Smara. What did Chibani care ? He was at home : I, lost . . . (they tried to explain that it would have been unwise to come into Tigilit with donkeys and the camel : that it would have excited attention, and so on. . . .)

At last, raising my head, I saw a star : Venus, in the dark sky, hardly above the shadowy wall of the ravine. And then we were at the top.

I hoped that was the end of my woes. Not at all. We had to keep on. We had to travel for perhaps another hour. I shall not attempt to say what I endured : rocks, and more rocks, and stones that lacerated my feet. Each time I thought we were there, we were pushed on again.

Finally, the barking of dogs. We came out of the stony bed of a oued and I saw the silhouette of two palm-trees in the dark. A minute or two longer and we came to a wall, to a door through which we passed. A huge courtyard, surrounded by low buildings. Walls. I slipped exhausted to the ground. I was dying to piss, but I had not even strength enough for that. A candle. I looked at my hands. They were almost black. My face was probably black, too : from exhaustion. Ultimately, I managed to piss, and then

[1] Finish : nothing doing.

went into an empty room, where I lay down. El
Mahboul, still a good sort, slipped his purple djellaba
under my head. I was tormented by a fearful thirst.
El Mahboul promised to bring me some water as soon
as Larbi caught up. How I wanted that water ! I
thought of the sea, of a cold-water tap, of beer . . .
but all the time I was half asleep, almost drunk with
exhaustion. Then I heard the camel. With what
keen attention I listened to every sound. I imagined
I heard some one pouring water. I fooled myself.
Then . . . it was true ! El Mahboul, stooping to
enter the low door, brought me half a teapotful, which
I emptied in three gulps : perhaps a pint and a half.
Then I ate a packet of chocolate. That made me
thirsty again. I heard some men, who came to greet
Chibani, in the courtyard.

' All right ? '

' All right, thanks ! '

' Then you're all right ? '

' All right . . . really all right . . . quite all
right ! ' and so on, as usual.

Soon, El Mahboul, who had scrounged some of my
chocolate, and probably discovered that it made for
thirst, brought me a little pot of water which found its
way into my stomach, to the last drop.

Then I stretched out for sleep. Roused by Larbi,
who brought me some tea. Then they made me eat
half a meat-cake, and then I lay down again in a
welcome sweat and slept with hardly any covering,
and not suffering the least trace of cold . . . a long,
unbroken sleep.

Now, how much better I feel : stiff, and my
stomach a little tender because of the quantity of

THE *BLED* TO THE NORTH OF DJEBEL TABAIOUT
SEPTEMBER 20, ABOUT 9.30 A.M.

DJEBEL AND OUED TIGILIT
SEEN FROM THE HOUSE OF LHASSEN

water that I drank ; but, to sum it all up : very
well.

* * *

They just interrupted me. Chibani has discovered
one of his friends, who has been laid up for nearly a
fortnight, after being shot in the mountains : leg
broken below the knee, the bullet having travelled from
side to side. I gave them some tincture of iodine in a
glass, and a little lint. And I hunted for words in my
Berber manual to tell them to be sure to clean the
wound thoroughly.

I am beginning to believe that ' *the baroud* ' is not
such a meaningless word.

* * *

Seven o'clock. We went into a nearby room, also
completely bare, while Bous swept the floor of the
other, and El Mahboul explained to me what our
future programme is to be, which brought a glow to
my heart : three or four days here, hiring *meharis* [1]
ordered by the sheikh, who is, if I understand aright,
a relative of Chibani ; seven days' march to Smara,
three days there ; seven days for the return ; five, six,
or seven days at Tigilit to rest the animals, &c. ; and
back again, with me still travelling as a man, on camel-
back, from Tigilit to Tiznit, making our journey by
night, while the women take the same road by day
and prepare our evening meals in readiness for us.

* * *

Wrote to Jean, to the caid,[2] Jeannie, relatives (I
believe that Larbi leaves to-morrow), after which I put

[1] Riding, or racing, camels.   [2] To caid Haddou.

things in order a little : medicine-chest, photographs,
&c.

Alone with Fatma Outana for part of the day.

El Mahboul returned and, as though he were saying
it was a fine day, announced :

(1) That one of our guards had recognized me for
a man.

(2) That the sheikh asks lots [1] and lots of money
before he will give me leave to go to Smara.

I asked him how much. He wrote down 30,000.
That sent the shivers down my spine, but El Mahboul
had his plan ready. The caid had definitely pro-
hibited payment of more than 15,000. Then Larbi
must go to Mogador, and if the caid and M. Jean
agree, and send the money, we will go. Otherwise
we will go back to Tiznit.

I howled ; I tried to put it clearly : ' *Makach flous,
makach Smara ?* ' [2]

El Mahboul confirmed my suspicions. I asked if
20,000, 15,000 would not be enough.

' No . . .'

' How much have you with you ? '

' Fifteen thousand. . . .'

I could not see how that happened. Probably he
had drawn on his own pay to meet the demands of the
people accompanying us, and for the animals and food.

Fifteen thousand ! At the worst, it only meant
adding another fifteen.

[1] ' Interrupted by Larbi, who offered me some bits of gazelle
on a spit—the first decent, tender meat I had eaten since leaving
Tiznit.'

[2] ' No money, no Smara ? '

I asked again :

' For that sum, will the sheikh guarantee me safe-conduct as far as Smara ? '

El Mahboul warmed up to it.

' No baroud. Camels, everything, as far as Smara and then to Tiznit.'

' All right, I agree. Give him the 15,000 that you have. Larbi is going to Mogador. My brother will give him 15,000.'

' And what about the caid ? ' asked El Mahboul. ' I have no authority to spend more than 15,000.'

I was annoyed. I rose, and shouted, throwing my arms about, thumping myself on the chest :

' *Je me fous du caid !* ' [1] (They all understand *je m'en fous !* and use it even when they speak in Arabic.) ' It is I, I (thumping my chest), who do the paying ! '

I grew so wild that I tore my clothes.

' *Enta, Larbi ; Tigilit, Mogador. Goul M. Jean flous. M. Jean gibb flous. Enta ; fissa, fissa, Tigilit. Ana, Mahboul ; fissa, fissa, Smara.*' [2]

That decided them. Then I explained to El Mahboul :

' El Mahboul, the caid told me I could trust you. Otherwise, you can be sure I should hesitate, &c. . . . but, since you say that with this extra 15,000 francs I can get to Smara, I do not hesitate.'

Larbi echoed, with conviction, ' *Je m'en fous du caid* ' [*sic*].

Just the same, we must stay here for five days, while the sheikh collects the guides, engages the camels, &c.

---

[1] Shall we say : ' To hell with the caid ' ?

[2] ' You, Larbi ; Tigilit, Mogador. Say to M. Jean, " money." M. Jean give money. You ; quickly, quickly, Tigilit. I and El Mahboul ; quickly, quickly, Smara.'

Monday, September 22.

[In this room] where I live entombed, confined, unable to put my nose out of doors, but free enough, within the four walls.

[Last night we came to an understanding with the sheikh.]

After yesterday's warning, I am always expecting the sheikh to change his mind, to increase his demands . . . but I cannot withdraw for 15,000 francs : our journeys and time lost, our plans broken ; return to Tiznit confessing failure : impossible. We must go forward.

2 o'clock.

This house : a courtyard surrounded by walls and small rooms not connecting with one another. The only light comes from a very low door. In actual fact it is not the house of Ali ou Boujma (that is the name of Chibani), nor that of his nephew (who has been to see me : a young Berber with a fringe of black beard).

The room where I am has a ceiling made of laths laid closely together and resting on solid trunks of palm-trees that have been roughly squared up : a yellowish, fibrous wood. Gun hung on the wall. In the niches of the walls, all sorts of things are kept : sugar, combs, slippers. They serve as cupboards. On the ground, a large mat which Chibani brought and spread. I sit on the pack-saddle of a camel.

This is where I sleep, eat unripe dates, gazelle on skewers, or cooked with a sauce that is invariably highly spiced, served, in this case, in a large blue-and-white enamel bowl, which it is amazing to find in such a place.

This is also where I write, where I dress the second toe of my left foot, whose sore, after granulating, has turned white and swollen, become very ugly.

Three or four times a day, mint tea : the four glasses, the tin quart-pot which Jean bought, the little enamel pot, the two teapots. The glasses are washed by pouring the same water from one to the other. The big teapot serves as a kettle. In the small one the tea is put, which is brewed with a very little water, which is poured off immediately. Then boiling water is poured in, and two or three large pieces of sugar and the mint is added. Then, a little wait, and some of the tea is poured out and tasted. A glassful or two is poured out and turned back into the teapot again. And at last it is offered to the party.

Here, Larbi says his prayers standing, then kneeling quaintly sideways. He bends to the earth, repeating his prayers like a priest, intoning with the same modulations and diminuendo . . . only breaking off to belch or scratch himself, or to take a backward glance.

* * *

The saucepan : they have just used it to water the camel.

* * *

The redemption of aimless days. . . .

Included in action ; part of the company . . . in the enterprise itself, where everything is authentic.

Here am I, dolt that I was during those slow, easy

years, agitated, tormented ; here am I at the point
where everything (the march ; the delay that is not
without purpose ; the sickening immobility under a
blue veil ; the dreary life circumscribed by four walls ;
the sores of my feet ; food taken from a camel's trough,
in which the women have washed their hands ; the
sprouting beard ; the little event of shaving, or of not
shaving ; the close watch over tongue and stomach ;
the care of my toes ; the mosquitoes ; the irritation
when the women make fun of me), where everything
serves for improvement, as coarse food nourishes a
ready body ; where everything is a new sustenance ;
where each day weighs heavily on me ; on us, because
the joy is double.   United by the same will, the same
power ; these multiple golden forces transfigure me,
transfigure him, my brother. A course determined
by our mutual will, which, in my journey towards
the goal, I seek to keep, and to transform from what
as yet is hazardous into certainty.

For it is you who must be reached : the place which,
once trodden, will give to our steps a lasting worth.
You alone, because we write our names in your
earth, can give weight and final shape to the effort,
bringing it out of the formless to the formed, acceptable
to us all.

No more of this and that—Dra, El Akhsas, and my
notes—but one name only which epitomizes them all,
sufficient unto itself, made for the ears and the mouths
of men : Smara.

* * *

[Larbi leaves at seven o'clock to-night, but will not
return here with the money ; that will be brought by

Muhammed, another brother of El Mahboul—a stout fellow, it seems, but whom I do not know. Chibani will go with Larbi as far as Tiznit and return to Tigilit with Muhammed.]

Tuesday, September 23. 8 a.m.

Last night, Larbi and Chibani [1] went. Then El Mahboul told me that the sheikh had decided to spread the rumour that the woman Boujma (myself) had gone with them, but that actually at ten o'clock, when night was well advanced, some one would come to take me to another house, where El Mahboul and the two women would join me with the baggage in the morning, making plenty of noise, going backwards and forwards, and taking care to be seen by everybody, so that nobody would think that there was any one else in the new billet.

I put on a well-worn, large blue tunic, the costume of the men of the country. They placed an enormous

---

[1] My brother gave them the notes already written, the exposed spools of films, and a letter in which he asked me to give Muhammed sixteen thousand francs.

He reassured me concerning his health. He asked me to see to the development of the films he was sending, to take note of the numbers of the spools and the order of each exposure on the rolls. He told me to send new rolls with Muhammed, as well as certain medicines and some tinned fruit. After outlining his probable programme, Michel arranged to meet me on October 17 by the Oued Massa, saying that he could only advise me of his return two or three days in advance.

I received the message on September 29.

Muhammed, to whom I gave the money and some provisions, left Mogador on October 4. After joining Chibani at Tiznit, he reached Tigilit with him. (Concerning the incidents of this journey, see pp. 153 and 157.)

turban on my head, and I went into the court. The night was moonless.

I was presented to the tall shadow of a man, who made me take off my slippers. Barefooted, I could not move. El Mahboul gave me a pair different from my own . . . which did not fit. Why?

The man took me by the hand, moving like a shadow by my side. In spite of all I could do, my slippers made a little noise.

We reached a tiny street flanked by houses. Here my guide made me remove my slippers. Throughout the journey I kept asking myself : ' Is this the nephew of Chibani, whose face I know quite well, or is it another man ? ' In the darkness I could not make certain. At the end of the alley, ending, I believe, in a cul-de-sac, we stopped before a door. My guide let go of my hand and groped about. Could not open the door.

He took my hand again. We retraced our footsteps. In the middle of the alley he paused before another door, pushed it open, and made me enter. I found myself in a narrow entry that was pitch dark. Before us, a door giving on to a courtyard.

The man said something : I understood him to mean that I was to stay where I was, and not to move. Then he went. I sat hunched up, close to the wall. I turned my head a little to the right, and faintly saw the earth of a courtyard. I thought I recognized wraps, and people lying there. A woman coughed. Animals, asses most probably, munched their barley. A fonduk? [1] I felt my left foot, afraid that the dressing I had put on might have come undone on the way. Happily, it was still there.

[1] Native hostel.

I considered my peculiar situation : led by a man whose face was hidden, and whom I did not know, through the shadows of the streets and houses which I could not see, whose shape, even, I could not perceive, inhabited by a fanatical people. And I recalled, why, I do not know, the fugitives of Poussin's *Plague in Athens*.

Suddenly, footsteps in the street. Then some one shook the door, opened it, and, behind me, some one entered and went into the courtyard. Not my guide, evidently. But if he had knocked up against me, spoken to me ? What a chance for him, when he saw that I did not understand ! A white man, with fair hair . . . good-bye to Smara ! Luckily, he did not even see me. I waited again. Was I to wait there until the dawn ?

Footsteps again. Some one pushing the door. A hand groping in the darkness. I thought it must be my guide. I rose and followed him. Once more we were before the door, and this time it was open.

I passed into a courtyard, which he made me cross to the foot of a staircase. I went up it, always followed by the man, to a small room, as dark as an oven. A room about eight or nine yards long and about two yards wide, divided into two unequal parts by a sort of partition wall of stone.

In the smaller, which was at the end of the room, the ground was completely covered by a mat and a coverlet with black and white stripes, soft to my feet. The man, by signs, made me lie down. In any event, it was the only position possible in that part of the room. The ceiling, made of laths blackened by smoke, was not high enough for me to stand erect.

The man left me, returning shortly. He sat beside me, put the candle on the ground between us, took a cigarette-holder, stuffed it with *kif*,[1] which he took from a skin-pouch, lit the candle, and puffed, or rather inhaled deeply, for five or six whiffs, put his smoke aside and lay by me. He spoke to me . . . I did not understand—' *man arf.*' [2]

He had taken off his turban to smoke. While he still had his mouth covered, in the light of the candle, with his small, piercing eyes, his high cheek bones, he was a veritable death's head, one of Dürer's villains.

I asked him :

' *Enta goul Amerikan ?* ' [3]

' *Oualou.*' [4]

He lay beside me. Then he made a sign, telling me to listen. The distant sound of tambourines and of hands being clapped together. He himself imitated the hand-clapping. I gathered that there was some festival going on.

I prepared myself for sleep. He touched me and, showing me the direction from which the noise came, made me understand that he was going to the fête. I indicated that I had comprehended his meaning, and that in the meanwhile I should sleep.

He rose, went to the other end of the room, and came back with a large vessel, shaped like a basin, with a raised base, and with a handle. On hands and knees I moved towards it, believing that he was giving me something to drink. Chuckling with amusement, he stopped me, and in sign-language explained its use : it was what they commonly used as a chamber-

---

[1] Native narcotic.   [2] ' I do not understand.'
[3] ' Do you speak American ? '   [4] ' None.'

pot. I laughed. He laughed. We laughed. And
he left me with a firm handshake, closed the door after
him, and turned the key. I blew out the candle and
lay down to sleep.

The new house was not so deep in the valley as the
one I had occupied previously : it was cooler, and I
felt a little cold.

I awoke at daybreak (not yet sunrise), which crept
in through the slits in the ceiling and the holes in the
wall. I sat up, stooping, and took a glance through a
hole in the wall that was slightly larger than the others.
I saw parts of small yards, round which were stones
and thorn-bushes, on which were thrown some striped
coverlets, drying, no doubt. Above the walls at the
end, the green heads of palm-trees, where magnificent
fingers of dates ripened. It was the Oued Tigilit,
which runs alongside the town. Behind the palm-
trees, the horizon was closed by the yellow, rocky
flank of the mountain. Unfortunately, the hole was
small, and it seemed hardly possible to take a photograph.

I was thirsty. At the other end of the room I
discovered a teapot, blackened by smoke : perhaps a
kettle. I took it up and, holding it close to my ear,
shook it. There was no water.

Returning to the carpet, I perceived between the
beams and the laths a number of objects : a wooden
spoon, the sheath of a dagger, covered with verdigris,
which somebody had slipped there.

I lay down again when I heard some one unlocking
the door. It was my guide. He offered me a large
enamel bowl full of magnificent dates, and then disappeared. How different from the unripe dates,

hard as bullets, which were my usual food during the days just ended, and which had made me believe that the good dates were to be found only in Paris. I ate a few too many ; but, never knowing when I may be able to eat or drink again, if anybody offers me either, I have only one idea : to devour as much as I can ; to gorge.

Then I heard the voice of El Mahboul, driving the asses into the courtyard. He climbed up to me with all my things. The women followed, and took their place in the other half of the room, near the door. Our host brought them a mat.

Talk with El Mahboul : he sang the praises of the sheikh. For these people, that man is really clever who is most adroit in scheming, giving as good as he gets, misleading his neighbours.

El Mahboul had bought and killed a goat, so that we should be well fed. Ate the liver, grilled on a skewer : excellent.

Less excellent : my foot, whose sore not only does not grow less, but seems to enlarge. With a needle, I extracted some pus, where the sore seems to have come to a head, and then applied iodargol.

The sheikh has said that if we have camels, it will be all right ; but, if there is a baroud : no camels.

I replied : ' We will go on foot.'

El Mahboul is confident. But what could I really do ? I might bandage myself well with mosquito-netting cut into strips. But would that be enough ? We shall have to do thirty or forty miles a day. If it were not for the question of water, and the heat, that would not be very formidable.

Wednesday, September 24. 10 a.m.

Lying on the mat, perfectly still, not even clearing
my throat, on account of our host's wife, who had
climbed up to the other room to drink tea (and has
not been told that I am here), come with her hairy
upper lip—I thought of an epic novel. The day of
sentimentality is over—the leavings of the nineteenth
and twentieth centuries. Why not locate it in the
sixth (Homer : some centuries after Achilles) ? Why
deny myself this poetic purification, this retrogression
in time ? *Hipparete* had some exaggerated sentimentality. And still, how I had fought against it.

What a perfect scheme for our lives : space . . .
our work in a score of directions . . . power ; assessors
of the Athenian Archons.

* * *

El Mahboul has gone to call on the skeikh. I told
him to ask how many women and children there are
in Tigilit. I know how many men there are : 135.
But it seems that the women and children are much
more numerous, the men being scattered here and
there on some mission or other. (More than 1000
women.)

Yesterday I made a French-Chleuh dictionary, to
enable me to talk understandably with El Mahboul.
I shall finish it to-day.

The sore on my toe having spread even more, I
dressed it with neat tincture of iodine. That burned
for a couple of hours, but I think the sore is now finally
cleaned. It would be a serious nuisance, should we
have to go on foot to Smara.

I am waiting impatiently for the return of the two messengers sent by the sheikh to see if we can get the camels.

I say nothing about the cooking (a parody on the real Arab cooking, which, they say, is original and good), except when something pleases me : skewers of meat, dates. But what sauces ! What meat-cakes ! What frightful barley bread !

12.30 *p.m.*
How curiosity is dulled by familiarity.
Stretched out on the rug. At the other end of the room, the two women squat, chopping up the kid, and, to pass the time, for sheer greed, spear large lumps of fat on spits and hold them over the flame, which raises an acrid smoke. The younger, in too much of a hurry to wait for the roasting to finish, presses the warm, melting fat in her hands, and licks her palms avidly.
And it seems quite natural to me. It has needed the greasy tongue of the girl. . . .

5 *o'clock.*
Three more days to wait, if all goes well. But it is long.
I am jailed here like a criminal. I have to use one of the communicating rooms as a privy . . . unable to go out.

The rooms are all alike : rough walls which crumble at the slightest touch ; smoky lath ceilings, so low that it is impossible to stand upright ; little holes in the walls to let in light (the size of a stone, no bigger).
I hold my nose at the holes ; all around : the near

MICHEL VIEUCHANGE IN SAHARAN COSTUME

AT TIGLIT. MICHEL VIEUCHANGE IN THE
HOUSE OF LHASSEN

mountain ; the girdle of palm-trees with such green heads ; little yards near by ; sometimes a man ; a woman ; bare children.

In the other rooms, where I go sometimes, jars are propped in corners, a camel saddle hangs from a joist.

My toe seems to be healing.

To-night I lay a long time before going to sleep. Thought a great deal ; of Smara in particular. It is imperative that I should succeed in reaching it. I feel myself ready for anything ; to walk for seven, ten days, if needs be.

I have conceived the beginning of the book ; but, naturally, since I have no light by which to write, I cannot recover that facility of words which must be caught quickly or it fades so easily. Only the dry bones remain—the thing is there, but it is not the thing.

A sort of preface, perhaps : we are two who have done this thing, even if only one of us has been able to reach Smara. This expedition was planned and executed by a team.

To give this mission a name : it is *a raid*.

Thursday, September 25. 7 *a.m.*

I had not understood that Chibani's nephew went with Chibani and Larbi, to go to the souk (probably El Akhsas, or Oued Noun) to buy barley, sugar, &c. He will be returning on Sunday.

Flies : flies and lice. The meat hanging above our heads covered with flies. They swat it every minute. A buzzing swarm.

From one of the windows I saw women in the courtyard erecting a tent : dark-skinned (liquorice) ; coal-
black hair, two plaits on either side of the ears, coming
together below ; blue veil on the head, leaving the
front hair free. On the hair, a sort of diadem or
bandeau with red-and-white designs. Necklaces and
bracelets with the same designs. Hanging on their
foreheads, a little square bag . . . most likely an
amulet.

1 *p.m.*

List of the people going with me to Smara : two
Reguibat sheikhs ; two friends of these sheikhs ;
Chibani's nephew (Ali or Muhammed) ; our host,
Afken Lhassen ; El Mahboul : eight, including
me.

Or perhaps : one Reguibat sheikh ; one of his
friends ; the sheikh of Tigilit [Ali or Mouloud] ; our
host, Afken Lhassen ; Chibani's nephew ; El Mahboul;
myself : making eight in all, just the same.

* * *

Deliberately, I will not imitate your diet of stone
    and bronze.
Deliberately, I will not impose on my body an
    absolute abstinence.
In the hope of this transfiguration.
Where do you go ?
Where do they go, with leaves in their arms ?
Let me have the sun, as I am.

.   .   .   .

My tastes are simple, simple.
My breathing light.

I will not cut myself off from others, assume another gravity, another nature.
Nor will I pursue the Divine Solitude.

* * *

Friday, September 26. Still at Tigilit. 3 *p.m.*
Lhassen, the owner, has just been to see us, not
exactly for the sake of our company : he comes to
scrounge what he can—sugar, tea, mint ; generally
all the lot at the same time.

I took the opportunity and pumped him a little.

He assured me that we shall have good meharis, and
that we ought to be able to reach Smara in three days,
travelling day and night.

. . . I have been explicit to El Mahboul, that,
unless it is absolutely unavoidable, I will not make the
journey in such a manner. I want to be able to stop,
and to work in comfort (purely a relative term). I
have insisted on a tent (how can I photograph the
kasbahs [1] at close range and without danger otherwise ?) . . .

He spoke of an island, Lmraïssa, where there are
Spanish traders. Tells me even of a drawbridge
raised at night. Is it Cape Juby ; is it Villa Cisneros ?

[I questioned him on the route to be travelled.]

Among the names which he mentioned, I found
only Fara already given me by Chibani.[2] Also called

---

[1] Citadels.

[2] Names given by Lhassen : Tigilit, Oued Dra, Gratlamir,
Fara, Chebaïka, Seguiet el Hamra, Reguibat, Smara.

On the sketch (page 100 *of note-book No.* 3*) from which I took these
names, Tigilit, Gratlamir, Fara, and Smara are shown as villages.*—ED.

Names given by Chibani : Zini, Farra (I am not always sure

Seguiet el Hamra the Oued Seguia, and suggested
that when we had crossed it we should still have
about ninety or a hundred miles to travel before
reaching Smara. That seems to mean that after we
have gone to the south we shall have to branch off
to the east (or the west). . . .

* * *

Photographed Tigilit from a hole in the wall (which
was very difficult to enlarge sufficiently for me to use
the camera).

5 *p.m.*

Lhassen has just brought me some cooked maize
in a little basin, and a piece of moufflon . . . all very
good.   At noon, I had no appetite for the remainder
of the goat.   Even when cooked, this meat has a
disagreeable smell.   El Mahboul and the women think
that excellent.

5.30 *p.m.*

Delousing, the best effort yet.

Saturday, September 27.   8 *a.m.*

This ought to be the eve of departure.

2 *o'clock.*

Ali, Chibani's nephew, got back from the souk about

whether these are names of districts, settlements, or tribes),
Telozone, Telaïnt (Aït Youssa)—many tents—Aït Chegoult,
El Arousiin, Izargiin, Ouled Delim, Seguiet el Hamra, Reguibat,
Smara.

(*For Gratlamir, Fara, Telozone, which it was not possible to identify,
the spelling of the note-books has been retained.*—ED.)

noon, with the camel and provisions (sugar, barley, soap, &c.).

3 *o'clock*.

Lhassen just came racing in, after mounting the staircase four steps at a time, gesticulating, and saying something which I could not understand. He took Ali's carbine and flew off, running hard, followed by Ali.

I learned from El Mahboul what had happened : the baroud. They have stolen some goats, or what not.

At about half-past two, I was able to wash myself all over. Last preparations for the journey.

They still eat this terrible meat.

Lhassen kindly brought me a large bunch of dates this morning, but they are not ripe. In taking them, incidentally, he has laid himself open to trouble, as it is forbidden to gather the crop for another fortnight.

Unable to eat the dates as they were, I stoned them and cooked them with a little water and sugar. Not too successful.

Mountains opposite : bare, with parallel ridges in circumvolutions, zebra-like striations, deep-brown. Mountains a clear, yellowish-brown.

5.45.

No news yet of the sheikh's messengers.

As I understand it, to-day he is entertaining a hundred and fifty men, coming from Aït Skiri with

sugar, barley, &c., and going about 125 miles beyond
Tigilit. So that El Mahboul, who was not invited to
the banquet, has no fresh news.

Have I said that the sheikh assured El Mahboul,
who really does look like a Roman, that in the Sahara
they would take him for a Spaniard, or an Italian?

Seeing me always flat on my face, sniffling in front
of a hole which gives me a view of the tents, the square
houses with a few windows, buildings round a large
courtyard, and of palm-trees and mountains, Bous
exclaimed, shaking her finger, ' *Kif-kif ouchen !* '
(which is to say : Jackal !).

Disappointed in El Mahboul.

Yesterday, when I asked him if he understood some
words of Chleuh which I pronounced, so as not to be
quite helpless on the journey and wanting to be sure
that he understood them, he replied at first, but ill-
humouredly ; then, not at all. When I insisted, he
said :

' Smara : work ! work ! Here, I am comfortable
with the little girl.'

Saying that, he stretched a foot across the knees
of Fatma Outana, who cracked his toes and scratched
the sole of his foot. That was how they passed their
day.

She ; dumb and scowling : he ; talking in a steady
stream to persuade her. Enough to make your hair
stand on end.

To-day, El Mahboul got himself a cup of goats'
milk. I asked him to get me the same.

' *Oualou* ' (There is none).

And he lay on the other side. That is only a suggestion of his humour to-day.

We will adjust that at Mogador. I am avoiding scolding, it has no longer any effect (twice only since we began). I am willing even to go so far as to put myself out if he asks me to fetch something, to work like a woman, or act as servant to an Arab. But the time will come, when we are away from here, when he will get exactly what is coming to him.

Am I right in speaking of these trifles? The annoying part is that they use up my paper. However; a sketch : Fatma and the toes !

It is nearly seven o'clock. Still no news of the messengers.

Last night, while I was lying down, I heard the noise of their merry-making ; hand-clapping and simple chants which I should like to have taken down. The sheikh entertained five or six families of Tigilit (Mr. and Mrs.).

Sunday, September 28. 7 *o'clock.*
Larbi should be at Mogador.
Nothing new with me. Guess my impatience.

10 *o'clock.*
Lhassen has been to call on us. As he squatted near to me, my toothbrush, the tubes of tooth-paste, and the shaving-cream sent him into a fit of laughter. I rubbed some of each on to his palm and his wrist. He smelt it and was full of glee.

Waiting, but still nothing happens.

Noon.

I have nothing to do but wait. I think of the epic work in snatches : a young man, a girl, side by side, naked, for the first time. A sensation they will never catch again. Undreamed of well-being. Fragrance. Yielding firmness of bodies. Coolness and relaxation.

1.15.

Still no messenger.

This is how the raid will be made : El Mahboul, Lhassen, Ali, the sheikh of Tigilit, and myself in one group, and preceded by another group, including the two Reguibat sheikhs and some others, who will clear our way. They will warn us if all is not well, and we shall forsake the road, change our direction, and go into the *bled*.

As for the rest, Lhassen says that they are all quite ready to shoot.

Where have I seen this head : Lhassen ? Not in Dürer. In Mantegna ? In any event, Lhassen is a type I like. Ali does not inspire the same confidence : small forehead, sidelong looks, knavish ; although he pretends to be mild and inoffensive.

* * *

I do not know whether I made a note of these symptoms of utter fatigue (after the gorges of Asder).

My legs and knees trembled like a foundered horse when I stood upright, without trying to move forward.

* * *

A raid ! That is exactly the description which I ought, which I like, to give to this crossing of the

Sahara to Smara. In spite of myself, the close con-
sideration of the route to be travelled outweighs in
importance any personal notes to be made. I do not
intend to ignore these, but I am getting ready, with
determination, to make a topographical survey as well
as I can. I shall keep a special note-book. My compass, my watch, the speed of the camel. The shorter
distances I shall judge by sight. I have in mind the
400 yards paced with Jean along the canal at Nevers.

6 *o'clock*.

Still nothing.

The sheikh has decided to go, even without the two
Reguibat sheikhs, it seems.

9.30.

Still no news of the messengers. El Mahboul has
gone up to see the sheikh.

I have now spent eight days here in this room, in
parts of which I cannot stand erect, where I have to
pick the places where my head will go without stooping, where the coverlet and the mats are full of lice.

Lhassen and Ali have just left us. The latter always
has a look of Judas. All four sitting round a single
candle, I asked them if there were many houses at
Smara.

' Like Tigilit,' they replied, but it was only from
rumour, because none of them has been there.

' How many days to reach Tindouf, Timbuktu,
Atar, and Senegal ? '

Lhassen wants me to hunt moufflon on the way back
from Smara.

Very proud, El Mahboul showed them Jean's watch,

opening it and showing the works. The others listened, and examined it closely.

In the same way, El Mahboul pushed the sketches of Fatma Outana, Bous, and himself under their noses, which I had scribbled on a blank page of Laoust. They found difficulty in deciphering the drawings . . . not used to it. Stared at them, holding the book upside down or on the side, ultimately recognizing a nose, an ear, an eye or something.

1.30.

Sleep impossible. Vermin. Enervating and lowering. Ahmed [1] not back yet. What is he doing ? Is he sleeping at the sheikh's? Has he only bad news to bring?

If I blow out this miserable candle, which I have just relit, I shall soon find myself lying on my back . . . or my side . . . not knowing where to put my head. Then . . . the pestilential vermin : legs, groin, &c.; then a draught. This discomfort : am I ill? My pulse is good. Perhaps too much tea, and not enough food. (A barley-cake, half a handful of roast maize, and that is all.) I asked Ahmed for some maize mush, but he would be damned if he worried about it. He feasts on high meat with the sheikh.

I think of what I am carrying through ; of Jean, Jeannie, and the rest. That brings me again to an even keel.

1.30 *or* 2 *o'clock.*

We have reached the 29th, then. It is my saint's day. Do we up-anchor and get away ? That would be a real festival.

[1] El Mahboul.

Monday, September 29.

Disheartening : Ahmed returned during the night, about two o'clock, and after talking to me about the sheikh, and his wife (at which I jeered), told me that we shall not be able to start in under five days.

What could I do, what could I say ?

I spent an hour over the explanation, and how I struggled ! The reason seems to be : the brother of one of the Reguibat sheikhs has been shot in the leg. But that might as easily last ten days. The only thing I may succeed in doing is to see the sheikh for myself, and even of that I am still uncertain.

2 o'clock.

Still have not seen the sheikh. Have made up my mind to have it out with him, but not to start until Thursday, in order to secure the protection of the two Reguibat sheikhs ; besides, if I drive them to an immediate start they may refuse to go, or at best obey unwillingly.

I wanted to sleep. Too many flies, too much vermin.

Accepting the inevitable, I amused myself in a delousing campaign, and this time I found a few well-developed specimens. Big and little, I suppose I slaughtered a couple of a hundred. I shall have to get used to them, and the expected is easily accepted. But then, I have expected everything, accepted everything. Still . . . !

The better to defend myself, I took off all my clothes (black tunic, pants, blue veil, and even El Mahboul's lilac djellaba, which I have appropriated), retaining only a large white shirt, which I examine continually : head in ; head out.

The women, Bous and Fatma, have been pulping some leaves, turn and turn about, in a crude sort of mortar placed between their legs, coating their hands with the pulp.   They looked as though they had been in a dish of spinach.   For half the day they kept them coated thus, even when handling flour and sugar. Then they scraped off the plaster, washed their hands in water, and the skin reappeared ; stained red.

4.30.
I have still not seen the sheikh.

.   .   .   .

They have amputated the leg, below the knee (too low and too late, most likely), of the poor wretch for whom I gave them some tincture of iodine a few days ago.   Ahmed came to ask me for some more, as well as for advice.

' It does not stop bleeding ?   Let them tie it tightly above the knee.'

' The wounded man, his wife, his brother, all cry for a little more of the brown liquid.'

' Here is something that will have the same effect : five tabloids of clonazone.'

I was sure that the Reguibat, and any other savages who heard of his good deeds, would give hospitality and right of passage to the physician and surgeon who found himself among them !

It is a question whether it would not be as well to send for Jean and a case of instruments.

Tuesday, September 30.   Morning.
The sheikh did not come last night, but sent his man Lhassen, to bring me a huge bowl of dates, some

of which were ripe (an indication that he wants to
keep on good terms with me), and to advise me that if
I am minded to insist on an immediate departure, we
can start to-morrow.

All that I had intended to say to the sheikh I said
to Lhassen. I had worked up a stream of words in
Chleuh which enabled me to be a little more fluent
and precise than usual.

This is what I said to Lhassen, when he, Ahmed,
and I were gathered round a candle, the two women
at a distance, in the dark.

' The sheikh put the delay first at eight days, and
then at five. There is no reason for that delay.'

Protests from Lhassen and Ahmed.

' . . . But no ! The sheikh's brother cannot be
well in five days. It may happen, like the man in
Tigilit, that they will have to cut off his leg. Then,
in five days, the sheikh will say : " Be patient, the
baroud is on." '

Lhassen : ' There will be no baroud. It is going
on now, on the other side of the Dra, not far from here,
but that will be over in three days.'

' Why three days ? '

' The people who started it will go. They never
stay more than a few days in the same place.'

So, taken all in all, it seems that in about five
days the chances of a good journey will be brightest,
because :

1. There will be no djouch [1] moving about in the
neighbourhood. But that does not mean that we
shall encounter no djich [2] before we reach Smara,

[1] and [2] : Raiding parties (*plural and sing.*).

or that on the return we shall not pass through territory
where raiders are at work. On the contrary, it will
be amazing, according to Ahmed, if we cover four
or five hundred miles, over a fortnight, without coming
within range of raiders. In that case, we shall change
direction, or go into hiding ; or, if we come across
them unawares, and the party does not seem too
formidable, we shall fight our way through. Should
the raiders be in force, then we must pay passage-
money (dangerous for me, signifying that the presence
of one of the Reguibat sheikhs means little as a
protection).

2. The two Reguibat sheikhs have said that they
would be in Tigilit in four or six days. And they
could be.

So I replied to Lhassen :

' I will be patient until Saturday, but on Saturday,
with or without the sheikh, we are on the march.'

' *Wakha* ' (That is understood).

' Does either of you know the way, as far as the
district where the two Reguibat sheikhs are now ? '

' The sheikh and I have already covered a good part
of the way. We will find the rest easily enough.'

' Can we go that way to Smara ? '

' Yes.'

' Very well, we will go that way. I will give medicines to the sheikh's brother, and the other sheikh, to
thank me for that, will accompany me to Smara.'

' *Wakha*.'

El Mahboul asked me :

' Could you cut off his leg ? '

' No, but I can give him medicines that will help to
cure him.'

I hesitated before taking this decision, wondering
if the sheikh of Tigilit were waiting for the return of
Muhammed, so that he could get the money and then
drop us.

That was why I named Saturday (before Muhammed
could have arrived). If on that day we have not
started, I intend, as I told Ahmed, to send some one
to stop Muhammed.

But El Mahboul tells me that the sheikh is acting
in good faith, and I think so, too.

There are phrases like ' Don't split hairs ' which
are so useful, sometimes, but which do not apply in
circumstances such as these. Why ? An inner sense
which prompts you. Just the same, I sometimes need
to remind myself of the patience of Cortés, for instance.
These examples are sometimes useful to us.

.   .   .   .

Every night, now, I look through one of the holes
at the women, going and coming round a tent with
brown and white stripes. One of them is not too bad-
looking : sometimes she leaves her right breast exposed
as she crouches to blow her fire, rises and walks with
a splendid lightness of tread.

But, Ahmed tells me, these women never wash.

10 o'clock.

Delousing. I suppose I killed about thirty of the
little beasts, but not a good one among them. Hardly
a trace of blood on my finger-nails. Yesterday I had
to stop frequently, to wipe off the grease and blood
of the victims.

Noon.

About an hour ago an Arab drove his flock of goats into the courtyard. The baroud, it seems, has broken out not far away, somewhere to the east of Tigilit, and the Arabs are driving their animals home, bringing their tents with them. One of our asses, and Ali's five camels are pastured down there.

Fatma Outana, with the same dull apathy, still scratches El Mahboul's feet. She, herself, a leg stretched out, rubs the sole and the toes of his right foot with the spout of the kettle—to which she puts her mouth to drink, as also do we. Montherlant would find that most intriguing.

The sore on my toe, which I wanted to heal quickly, has opened at the side. I have cut strips of mosquito-netting, which served as packing for my medicine-chest, and wrapped my feet. If I have to walk to reach Smara, perhaps an improvement on this dressing will minimize the pain.

* * *

The baroud was about 10 miles from Tigilit, and began with daybreak. There were several killed and wounded. Among the killed is Ali's brother-in-law, who died at about eight o'clock.

5 o'clock.

The sheikh's brother was killed. The assailants belong to the Aït Lhassen, from the neighbourhood of Goulimin. More than three hundred camels were taken, and nobody knows how many goats and tents. That took place in the neighbourhood of Gir.

There is not a man left in Tigilit. The widows of
the men who were killed are raising their lamentations.

Wednesday, October 1. Morning.

The second wound which opened on my second toe is
not so good this morning . . . somewhere about the
size of a sixpence. The first seems nearly healed.

Delousing. The louse lies on the sacrificial stone of
my thumb and I crush him. My finger nail is like an
ancient altar, greasy and bloody.

The men of Tigilit want to take the warpath against
the Aït Lhassen, but only in a month's time. In the
meanwhile, the sheikh will go with me to Smara :
' *In sh'allah.*' [1]

Our donkey (the one I nearly always rode) was taken
by the Aït Lhassen, and carried off with the rest of the
booty.

The man of El Bordj, who came upon us so suddenly
by the lake, just when I was going to drink, and who
later brought us to Tigilit, was killed yesterday noon.
It was he who had seen that I was a man in woman's
clothing. Through the opening of my veil, I had observed him for a few seconds : only a boy, seventeen
years old, maybe, very proud of his rifle.

Noon.

No word of the sheikh or of Lhassen. Is this baroud
going to last for ever ? They have asked El Mahboul
to lend them our remaining ass, to bring in the
wounded.

[1] ' If God wills.'

1 *o'clock.*

Ahmed, called on for help, pretended to be ill.

Ahmed bought a goat for fifty-five silver francs. It was slaughtered in the courtyard.

This, I think, is a lodging-house : Lhassen, the Negro, another Arab.

While this inaction is forced on me, I can at least profit by the experience of complete isolation, and live in the past and in the future. My poor little diary in hand, I try to revive this or that day of a year that is gone . . . and my memories are so powerful that for a while they override the present. Or perhaps it may be that wonderful future . . . if only God lets us live.

8 *o'clock.*

Time could hardly be said to speed merrily here. Difficulties increase in the way, constantly postponing our departure. The baroud. Uneasiness about Lhassen, the sheikh, the immediate results of this fighting. And it has started to rain. It rains heavily, it seems, about forty miles away, and it may happen that the Dra will be unfordable. All these things, this interminable delay, make me a nervous wreck. At the end of my resistance, there are times when I grind my teeth, when I can see myself clawing the ceiling, head downwards, like a fly.

My imagination is too vivid. (Quite willingly I let it become so, thinking that I must work, be constantly alert.) Then I was compelled to stay here, and now I visualize the difficulties too much. I become dispirited, and too often say to myself : if the sheikh is killed ; if this ; if that, what must I do so that I finally reach my goal in spite of everything. I turn the questions over and over again. I fumble with half a dozen solutions : wait for the return of Chibani, who at least knows part of the way, &c. &c.

But an hour ago, happily, while I picked one of the bones of the goat, sitting behind the partition wall, El Mahboul and the two women were entertaining Lhassen's wife and her moustache in the other part of the room—plunging their hands in turn into the saucepan, and belching—and Lhassen himself arrived.

What satisfaction there was in hearing his voice ! And it was not only the satisfaction of finding my guide again ; the simple fact that he was safe and sound stirred me more than I believed possible. When his wife went, I left my corner and saw him sipping his tea. We shook hands for a long time without speaking. What a fine sort he is ! He understood that I had been uneasy, and he showed me that he appreciated my thought. Then he gave me a little information. The Aït Lhassen numbered about a hundred, including thirty horsemen. Three of these had been killed, and on them they had found Spanish (?) rifles, whose magazines carried clips of five cartridges. Of the Aït Bouhou, seven were killed, including the sheikh's brother, Ali's brother-in-law, the young man of El Bordj, and three wounded. The second warrior who had accompanied us here had thrown away his rifle and fled.

Lhassen himself brought me three glasses of tea and then left to rejoin his wife.

Thursday, October 2. 7.30 a.m.

The sheikh came to the threshold of the door this morning, while I was asleep, my head under the piece of white cotton cloth that serves me as covering. He is still decided to start during Friday night. Unfortunately the sky is still cloudy.

.   .   .   .

We shall start our journey on St. Francis of Assisi's day. That makes me think of the other. Like him, I can say : Smara, town of our illusions. . . .

4 p.m.

Rheumatism (neuralgia in the dental nerves), following the cold nights of the Oued Noun. Enteritis.

* * *

He who has no doubt of the issue, even during the effort. . . .

Sad hours that I passed at Marseilles, on the boat. I have not yet confessed it ; but I was really afraid that I should not be able to succeed. What satisfaction warms my heart, what glow goes through me, when I think of where I am, where *we* are now—driven like a wedge into action, into the thing itself. Well home. A few more blows with the hammer and we shall be through. When the wedge is carefully withdrawn, we shall have turned the trick.

There is a trick in it, the trick of the acrobat, and it is done on the tight-rope. One runs, to prevent breaking his back.

What importance there is in a good beginning : the reliable man ! Then everything follows : another

man and another man. Men are the pieces in the
game.

I am like a rider in the mountain passes at night.
I trust myself to my mule. I have picked a good mule.
A little pressure on the reins, perhaps, a little steering ;
but done wisely.

5.30.

For a long time I was flat on my stomach in front
of a hole in the wall, scanning as much of Tigilit and
its surroundings as I could with my glasses. The
oued ; whose course could be recognized by the green
of the palm-trees—a green sprouting in tufts, where the
clusters of dates, almost ripe, make a touch of golden
yellow. Near the oued, two or three substantial
houses, one of them belonging to the sheikh ; simply
four walls of unbaked earth. The mountain, close
to the foot of which the oued flows along its winding
course ; yellow peaks, or maybe slightly rose-coloured,
with brown seams. Here and there flecked with
brown rocks.

Night of Thursday/Friday. 2 a.m.

About an hour and a half ago, towards midnight,
wakened by a shout from Bous (we were all sleeping
on the mat, Bous before the open door). I sat up,
and in the faint light beyond the doorway (the moon
was rising) saw just the head and shoulders of a man
(the steps of the staircase are of such a size) : Lhassen,
who spoke in a low voice. Ahmed went nearer, and
they talked, the while I was bathed in a sweat of
apprehension. What had happened ?

El Mahboul reassured me at last. The Reguibat

sheikh had just come in with two meharis, and it was
simply to bring me the news (I had asked to be advised
immediately) that the sheikh of Tigilit had sent
Lhassen. I breathed again.

Just now, I wanted to sleep, but Bous carried on
an interminable conversation with El Mahboul. After
bearing it for an hour, irritated, I asked El Mahboul
to be quiet, but that old hag of a Bous chattered worse
than before. I threatened to get busy if they did not
shut up. They did not shut up, so I lit the candle
and began to write.

I forgot : About eight o'clock, when we were already
lying down, Lhassen called for a few minutes, to tell
us that one of the most important tribes of the Aït
Youssa will open warfare against the Aït Lhassen of
Goulimin in three days' time. That will not alter
our plans in the slightest, which is all that matters.
The Aït Bouhou are close friends of the Aït Youssa.

Friday, October 3.   6.30 a.m.

Ali has just been in with the same mask of a face.
He asks Ahmed if I want to penetrate the walls of
Smara. Positively !

9.30.

The women are pounding the maize which will be
our staple food on the journey.

3 p.m.

El Mahboul came back from the sheikh's, where he
had had a meal with the Reguibat sheikh, who does
not seem to be very agreeable : ' I don't care about

money,' he said. ' I have plenty of camels and goats.
I don't want to bring a *roumi* [1] into my country.'

The sheikh of Tigilit, however, was able to persuade
him to go on.

The country as far as Smara is by no means safe.
We shall have to dodge about, and avoid the roads.

Neither the sheikh of Tigilit, Lhassen, nor Ali is to
go with us. There will only be the Reguibat sheikh,
a sheikh of the Aït Chogout (a neighbouring and
friendly tribe to the Reguibat), El Mahboul, and
myself. We shall travel mostly at night. For the four
of us, two meharis—one a female on the point of
giving birth.

The Reguibat sheikh asked what I was going to do
in his country :

' American trader, who wants to sell you sugar and
cartridges.'

We leave to-night, at ten o'clock. At last !

3.30.

I have decided to leave my notes and exposed films
here with the women. We ought to be back at
Tigilit—counting six days on the outward journey, two
days there, and six days for the return—by October 17.
If we are not back by the 21st, Muhammed will go to
Mogador, taking the notes and films. [2]

Lhassen's wife introduced.

[1] European.

[2] For my instruction, my brother added the following sugges-
tions :

' To Jean : You can wait about another five or six days without
worrying. If I should be captured, I will do my best to let you

7.15.

Final preparations. The meat, which smells a bit high already, in a linen bag. The maize flour rammed into a hairless skin, with a wooden pestle. Myself browned with permanganate.

El Mahboul develops a fit of homesickness. Danger? Leaving Bous . . . or, more particularly, Fatma Outana ? (This stinking meat.)

I was forgetting the new clothing, typical of the Sahara : everything blue. The veil round the head and neck makes a sort of helmet, reminiscent of the Middle Ages ; the protector for the nape of the neck, cloth to wrap over the mouth, and the big blue tunic are equally of the same period.

know by one of the men of Tigilit—Chibani, for instance. If I should be wounded, and you find it imperative to join me, do so cautiously. As a woman, as I did, I think. Stain your face and limbs. Travel preferably by night. With Chibani rather than Lhassen, Larbi, or Muhammed (all reliable). He is a clever old fox. Follow the advice of the sheikh of Tigilit (after that of the caid Haddou).

' Bring plenty of medicines (bandages, iodine, lancets). With them, you can travel anywhere, once it is known.'

III

THE FIRST ATTEMPT

Saturday, October 4.

[Written during the 6 o'clock halt, continued at the 10.30 halt.]

[Last night, Lhassen had not arrived at ten o'clock.] By the light of a candle, the women still sifted the flour. They packed the salt, meat, and my own belongings into two large sacks. Lying, sitting, I waited until midnight. Neuralgia. I slept a little. About midnight, Lhassen came to look for the packets. Long wait. Why? Was it because there were women jabbering in the courtyard?

At last, Lhassen again. Descent to the courtyard. Bous acting as scout in the alley. We crossed a sort of enclosure. Palm-trees. The oued.

Lhassen, who had handed me his own tattered slippers but had taken mine, made me remove them, and I had to walk for about half a mile along the river-bed in bare feet. River-bed full of stones, but I ought to add that I did not suffer too much on that account.

We followed the dry bed of the oued, each one carrying a load, of which mine (the skin of maize flour) was by no means the lightest.

Ultimately we arrived near to four men who were sitting on the ground. By the light of the moon, I

recognized El Mahboul, and Ali's treacherous face.
The two others, brigands both, were my new guides :
the sheikhs.

Standing for a moment beside the group, one of the
sheikhs said a few words which El Mahboul translated.
The sheikhs were bidding me welcome.

' *Salaam aleykoum.*' [1]

My reply, naïve as it was, brought them out of their
antagonistic silence. They smiled. At that moment
I had a strangely clear perception of what our determination to reach Smara had involved. Here were
two men who had already done about two hundred
miles, and were going to do three times as much,
because, in Paris, we had willed it.

I lay on the hard stones, after rebandaging my foot.
The sheikhs went to the other side of the oued, taking
El Mahboul with them.

Alone : lying with my face to a sky whose extent,
in Paris, is obscured by the works of man ; but there it
was possible to understand de Foucauld, seeking a God
at all costs : Muhammed, or Jesus.

Mosquitoes. Roomy clothes, where one can hide
from them completely.

The noise of camels, preceded by their strong smell.
There they both came, led by Ali. Quietly, he sat
beside me, without a word, then touched my bag
(roomy, with two pockets : one for the compass,
special note-book for directional bearings, and a pencil
always ready ; the other for the watch), and gently
drew it towards him, envied it, asked me for it.

' For Larbi,' I said, and he did not press.

(At this moment, while I write, my poor bag has

[1] ' Peace be unto you.'

just reached the hands of the Aït Chogout sheikh, who, in exchange, and without so much as a ' by your leave,' has slipped me his own, worn and old, not so convenient.)

Lhassen, who should have brought back my binoculars, did not reappear. Like a good scrounger, he borrowed them yesterday, to show them to the sheikh of Tigilit. I knew perfectly well that he had dispensed with the formalities of farewell. It made me furious at the moment, but that is over.

At last, at two o'clock, El Mahboul came back to me, and told me to follow the camels. Instead of driving straight south, we are to make a detour to the east, to avoid a dangerous road.

A long march, but not too difficult, until six o'clock. I watched carefully to see where I was going, and where best to put my feet. The moon disappeared, and it grew dark. Then the sun rose, slowly, because we were following the valleys.

Towards the dawn, a ravine, and water, heralded by the croaking of frogs. They drove the camels among the rocks at the end, towards some puddles of stagnant water. The Reguibat sheikh went from one to the other, tasting each and selecting the better water. I drank from the water-skin, which was nearly empty. El Mahboul had helped himself abundantly first, and the water in the pools seemed so putrid (just the same, that is what I am drinking freely now).

Along the way, I walked last, in the dark, finding it easy to read my compass, but my watch became impossible, trying to compute the size of the valley,

the height of the mountains. I have just entered a
few figures.

I got out the two cameras, kept one, and gave the
other to El Mahboul. We began our march again.
The sun was hardly up, but I took one or two photographs.

I could examine the faces of my sheikhs. The
Reguibat : bare-headed, long back hair, and beard.
The other : short front hair ; smaller, less beard. Both
obviously chary of me. Prompted by El Mahboul,
I recited the prayer I learned while pacing rue
Clapeyron.[1]

The effect was excellent.

' *Shwia marabout*,' [2] said the sheikhs.

Then we changed our direction, and instead of
travelling east, we moved towards the south, crossing a
range of hills which gradually increased in size.
Desert-like, the mountain : rocks greenish or ruddy or
brownish, all of flaky stone.

We marched steadily forward. Not for a second did
I stop. I took three photographs. Then the compass ;
the watch.

The sheikhs moved evenly, at great speed. Hard
going, sole of my slipper half unsewn. At the end,
El Mahboul and I were well behind. They waited for
us. We had a few minutes' rest (El Mahboul took a
picture of me), then I rode one camel and El Mahboul
the other.

Saddle perched high, on the baggage ; the various

---

[1] The Chehada : ' Ashhadou anna la ilaha ill' Allah. Ashhadou anna Muhammed, Rassoul Allah. Salla 'Ilah alayhi wa
sallem.'

[2] Little saint.

speeds of the camel ; unbelievably hard on the stomach.

Instinctively I tried all the positions you see in pictures : legs crossed. I sat firmly enough for me to plunge my hand into my bag, which hung from the pommel of the saddle, whose point was between my legs, and get my watch, compass, and note-book, and even to take a photograph of El Mahboul, who rode a little ahead of me.

As soon as we stopped, I drank. My mouth was dry the whole time, so dry that it hurt considerably to pronounce one word : ' Ahmed.' I waited minutes before making the attempt.

We followed a valley with orientation to the south. Thorny shrubs here and there.

Always the same dry mouth. El Mahboul gave me the half of an onion.

Towards 10.30, we stopped. The same stony valley. One side fell sheer, about eight feet high. A little shade. I do not know why, but they made me lie down twenty yards away from the others, in the shade, but in a very uncomfortable spot—stones, brambles— where I began to write.

. . . They have just fetched me to have something to eat. Tea, water, a piece of goat (they have moufflon but perhaps they think it is not high enough yet), and a good dish of maize. . . .

Work to do again ; a blinding headache.

When they were about to move on, they exchanged my clean clothes for rags (lice ?). During the noonday rest, a sort of white djellaba thrown over me, like a holy man. Writing difficult, since they make me lie prone, or nearly. There is no longer any shade, and the sun is devilishly hot. It is noon.

3 p.m. halt. [*Oued Dra, place called Tourg.*]

Started again at a quarter to one, still riding the camel. At times, perfectly comfortable, I could work easily, with camera, compass, and watch. But I had to be careful of the descents, even when slight : the camel broke into a trot, and there was the chance of a fall unless I hung on to the saddle. Wide valley, or pebbly plain. From time to time shrubs or small thorny trees. Not a man. Camel-droppings in quantities, indicating places where tents had been pitched.

Wide plain. Very hot wind, but agreeable. From my seat on the camel, the semi-intoxication which these Moors must experience : travelling in solitude ; wind ; scorching sun ; the lanky steed under them ; bare feet on the soft hair of the animal's neck; good seat ; movement always the same, rocking, pleasant because it never changes ; and a gun, of course.

And suddenly I thought : ' There will be dried meat without salt, days in the wind, some water.' [1]

On the bounds of the horizon, two large ranges with contours resembling various animals : hippopotami squatting. About three o'clock we reached the

---

[1] Recollection of a phrase which my brother wrote four years earlier, in a narrative still unpublished, *Hipparete*. ' Some time, he too (Alcibiades) would have a bare-backed horse, a bow, javelins, space, the aridity of the plains, days spent riding in the wind, men to hunt down and kill ; in the evening a tent of hair, meat without salt and dried, some water.'

SOME HOURS FROM TIGILIT
OCTOBER 4, ABOUT 5.30 A.M.

OUED DRA (TOURG, OCTOBER 4)
POOLS AND TAMARISKS

foot of these black,[1] treeless mountains, with horizontal seams rising to about half-way up, then eroded.

At the foot, the Oued Dra, which still had large pools of water ; sand ; clay, whose surface was covered with small cracks ; reeds on the water's edge. El Mahboul went in. I contented myself with a drink and photography : caution was advisable, near to water, which is so likely to attract people.

The camels grazed here and there on green shrubs. We sat on the flank of a hill, composed as usual of crumbling black stone. The sheikhs made tea.

I learned of a misfortune : the caid's camera was broken. Luckily both cameras take the same films.

5.15.

We took the road again half an hour ago, going slowly on foot, keeping a course to the south-west. According to El Mahboul and the sheikhs we shall have done at least forty miles. Utter weariness.

Sunday, October 5.

About 10 *a.m., during the ascent of Djebel Ouargziz.*

Last night, we travelled until eight o'clock, at first on foot, until nightfall, then on the camel.

On foot : wide plain, sandy or stony, bordered by parallel ranges of hills—to the left, black and steep, with horizontal crest, the sides a black wall ; in the distance, to the right : round, conical hills. The plain makes a bed for a tributary of the Dra.

. . . I was on the other side of the Dra ! I looked

---

[1] A black scale, the ' desert glaze,' is found on most of the rocks in the Sahara.

PHOTOGRAPH TAKEN FROM DJEBEL OUARGZIZ, TOWARDS THE NORTH

TRIBUTARY OF THE DRA IN THE VALLEY.   OCTOBER 5, ABOUT 9 A.M.

I asked El Mahboul for my medicine case, to make a new bandage.

' *Oualou*,' he replied, ' to-morrow morning.'

(I knew perfectly well that in the morning there would be no time to spare.)

I lay on the sand, with nothing on my head. The sweet stillness of the night ; neither cold nor hot. I drank from the water-skin, raising it above my head as I lay flat on the sand. To keep well here, it is necessary to drink all the time.

On the sand ; good bed for the first time for ages. I needed it. I slept soundly.

Wakened at 2.45. Good moon. The sheikhs were already making tea over a wood fire. They had also prepared a saucepan of maize with arganier oil.

However, the moon sank slowly, and darkness spread over the earth.

We began to move on again in the dark, on foot. Stony hillocks, covered with brush. Feet numb and swollen. All the weariness of last night. Slippers too big and worn, in pieces : I took El Mahboul's. To add to my troubles, I had to get out my compass from the cumbersome satchel below my hampering pile of clothing.

[1.15 *p.m. halt.   Place   called Amezera.*]

On camel-back throughout the night, till daybreak. Plain with some small hillocks. The camel, which refused to go farther, lay down, and swung his long neck round, threatening my legs with his teeth.

We reached a lake. Country where delays are

dangerous. Many tents, and no friends of the sheikhs. I took two photographs. The camels drank. We refilled the water-skins. I drank.

On camel-back. Tomb of a marabout (large pile of stones). Many tombs.

We travelled at speed to the right, towards the djebel Ouargziz. Dismounted, and began to ascend. Climb which lasted perhaps an hour and a half. Long clothes which hampered the feet. El Mahboul was all in ; so was I. The two camels jibbed, showing fright. Three photographs of me and one of the plain seen from mid-ascent. A camel, absolutely refusing to move, was led by the nose, by hand.

Stop for half an hour. Hidden under an overhanging rock, I wrote the beginning of this. Then some one called me.

The other side of the mountain, sloping gently down. Vast plain. Tents which I could not see. They must smell them, to avoid them in such a fashion !

On the camel until half-past one. Fatigue. Lameness which demanded all my will-power. I made an enormous effort, and always, always, we kept going : whither ? To the Tree ? No !

The camel always too much to the left.

At last, we halted beside a bush [Amezera].

I could do nothing more than stretch myself out, absolutely beaten. Drink ! Drink !

A little sleep. Awakened by the arrival of cups of tea . . . then a little work. Reloaded the camera and made notes.

They got under way again. My foot coming to a head, my back bruised.

In the midst of the climb, one of the sheikhs turned to me saying, ' It is hard, very hard. Would you like to go back to Tigilit ? '

He has conjunctivitis, wants me to treat it.

Example of what we are going through : the same sheikh (due to the sun, no doubt) suddenly had a spasm of nose-bleeding. Just the same, they are built of the real stuff, these fellows. Untiring.

Monday, October 6.
5.30 *halt.* [*Place called Liajerin.*]

Yesterday we moved on again about five o'clock and kept going till eight o'clock. Plain. Sand. So weary that it was akin to pleasure. Dragging one foot after another : sudden strains to get up : when one stumbled over a stone. Keeping going : following. [All that matters] not weariness, but the course travelled. In five days, Smara !

The dying sun. Tombs here and there, which move me. Why, I cannot say. The moon ; effacing the stars from half the sky. The flies cease their torment when night falls.

Good sand all the way, either hard (which is very good) or somewhat softer. Half-way, the sheikh sensed water behind some bushes. A hand lifting water to a mouth. Feet in the damp sand, right up to the ankles.

About eight o'clock ; halt. Fine sand. [The Aït Chogout sheikh complained of his foot : he had picked up a thorn.] Under the djellaba ; match, then candle. Needle. Then I spread my medicine chest, throwing away what was broken. On the wounds, a little iodargol and vaseline.

Coming near to me ; a scorpion, killed by El
Mahboul. No kettle ; it attracts snakes. (Two
killed already.)

To the left ; some low hills parallel to the route we
followed. To the right ; a plain stretching to the
horizon.

The sheikhs show more confidence in me (stovarsol).
Stretched out, I slept.

At one o'clock, reawakened and made a start.

Unbearable pain in my right heel. I hoped it
would pass. I walked for an hour. (The indisposed
sheikh and El Mahboul rode the camels.) Plain
everywhere, except that, half an hour after we started,
there was a single mountain to the left. Real desert ;
but fortunately flat.

An hour after the start, agonizing pain. Camels
afar off. I caught up with them.

On the point of being sick, and almost fainting.
Flat on the earth, with my bag pushed away from
under my head. What is the matter ? On my leg
and thigh there is a painful streak. Scorpion ? But
I had felt nothing. Anthrax ? I rubbed my leg,
blue from the stain of the cotton cloth. Match : no
line. Stretched a little. Teeth chattering. Cold.

Then, camel. Carried by El Mahboul. Made a
stirrup bandage of my clothes. Just escaped fainting.
Water. That was better.

Continued on the march until half-past five. Sand
and water. Star on the right, then overhead. Halt
[Liajerin].

Sun. I compelled myself to look at my foot.
Ordinary sores, puffed up. I cleaned them with
clonazone. Extracted pus. Vaseline : bandage.

SOUTH OF THE OUARGZIZ
OCTOBER 6, BETWEEN 7.30 AND 10 A.M.

ASCENT OF THE EASTERN SLOPE OF THE VALLEY SOUTH OF LIAJERIN
OCTOBER 6, ABOUT 3 P.M.

Hardly ate : maize, last of the chocolate, tea. That seemed better.

10 o'clock halt.

Camel. Improvised sort of sling to hold up my foot. Still often painful. No longer crossing level plain ; pebble-strewn undulations instead. Heaps of stones (photograph). Fresh camel-tracks. Sheikh uneasy. Country not safe. However, decided not to travel quite so fast.

Inclined to the west. Valley with rocky sides in view (photograph). After the camel had entered the valley he leapt from rock to rock.

Covered a little of the valley and came to a halt about ten o'clock. They found a place for me under an overhanging rock, about two feet above the surface of the earth. I slid under. Warmth. A little drowsy. Foot not paining me so much. Headache. Hands burning. Pulse 106 (thermometer broken), in spite of a dose of quinine taken two hours previously. I put it down to the sores.

Tuesday, October 7.
[8.40 *halt.*]

Yesterday : pulse rose to 115. Body feverish. Typhoid ? Anthrax ? No black veins. Undoubtedly malaria. And the fever yielded finally to two doses of quinine.

No sun. Heavy weather. Birds with a wide wing-spread crying as they soared over the valley.

Washed my foot in cold water (four sores). Finished the reel in the camera and reloaded. Took a little tea.

The valley through which we travelled was the

camping-ground of 5000 Reguibat only five days previously.

Started about half-past three. Camel. Fever. We followed the valley. Saddle too far forward and to the right. Fever lessened gradually, and went.

It became necessary to leave the valley. Ascended the djebel, riding the camel. Near the top, the saddle slipped sharply sideways, and turned over. I hung on. El Mahboul came and took me in his arms, got my foot out of the stirrup. The camel did not wait, but ran on. Three hundred yards to cover before I caught him up. El Mahboul had not fixed my saddle properly, because of which my going was uncomfortable in the extreme.

We then came to an undulating plain. Stones or rocks now and then. On the far horizon, straight ahead and a little to the left, a white range which caught the light of the setting sun.

Night, and moon. After the plain, we found ourselves facing a sort of ravine which led to another valley, and which we descended. Hard. Prone on the saddle, left elbow propped on the back, right hand on the pommel.

Then we worked south again, and followed the valley.

About eight o'clock, we stopped. I thought, and so did El Mahboul (since the camels were left loaded) that it was for a few minutes only. Actually, it was for the rest of the night.

These two sheikhs are savages. Always dumb, or practically so. Never known to laugh, except for once or twice when I narrowly missed cracking my skull.

Cold night. I curled up like a dog, limbs folded up. Hard earth. Foot.

Awoke about half-past six. Camel missing : hyena? They found it. We started.

Saddle never properly fixed.

At eight o'clock, halted near water. I reloaded the camera. Started again, this time with saddle properly mounted ; comfortable seat. We travelled until twenty to nine, always following the valley oriented south-west, or due west, and covered with thorny bushes or shrubs ; trees once in a while.

Water was frequently to be found, but, from to-morrow, I believe, we are likely to have to travel two days without water.

My foot : ankle swollen and four sores in very bad shape. Stabbing pains.

[*12.15 p.m. halt.*]
1.15 *p.m.*

From the bushes where I wrote that, I heard El Mahboul call me near the sheikhs. At most of the halts I do not stay in the same place, but at about twenty yards' distance. El Mahboul tells me (at least, so I understand) that that is done to avoid chance meetings with Arabs. But is it not because they would prefer to be alone?

Near the sheikhs, I arranged my medicine-case, and put the photographs into some sort of order. Then I dressed my foot (I could not stand upright for two minutes ; El Mahboul hoisted me on to the camel) and that of the sheikh. Then I ate a little maize. The Reguibat sheikh, very inquisitive, saw the little wallet from Fez in my satchel. I read the two names of friends of Merebbi Rebbo.[1] That seemed to impress them favourably.

.   .   .   .

We started again at about a quarter to eleven. Valley with westerly direction. After three-quarters of an hour it opened on the west to a wide plain ; but we did not go so far, taking another valley towards the south, which opened from the one we were following. We continued along this new valley until about a quarter past twelve, halting at a point where it ended in a cul-de-sac, travel during the day being limited because of the possible appearance of raiders.

The thought of the ascent causes me some misgiving. Here again, I must keep my distance : I am with El Mahboul under a bush, the sheikhs thirty yards away under a little tree. Sun ; then clouds ; sun ; wind. The hard earth ; thorns ; the dull ache in my heel.

If I did not make these notes as we go, everything would be blotted out, or nearly so ; or, if I wrote something later, trusting to my memory, it might be totally different. Day follows day, and I hardly notice them.

On and on ! Toiling, sticking like a leech to the saddle of a camel, trying to see if it is south or south-west, west, or east. Forcing my attention to the direction of the mountains, to the nature of the earth, remembering the water . . . here . . . here. . . .

[1] Names given to my brother by a certain Sidi Saïd, who now lives at Mogador. This former agent of Manessmann has maintained many connexions in the Sous and the locality of the Oued Noun.

Driving myself to take two reels of pictures each day (although with only one camera working). I photograph the important stretches. At night, I must be content to make mental notes, and to transcribe them at the end of the run.

Often I hunt in the satchel (in front, or behind), hanging on with the other hand. The camera is focused and the picture taken as best may be. Then I put it back. During this time the camel has gone to the left, and has to be brought into line again.

Or perhaps it is the ' see-saw,' [1] for which I hunt at the bottom of the bag—among the quinine, aspirin, watch, three note-books, wallet, clonazone, vaseline, unexposed films, and camera. Finding it, I strive, in spite of the jolts, to read the direction. Morning and night, when it is very low, I take direction from the sun for preference.

At the end of the stage, the directional note-book comes out at once. Effort to discover the name of this mountain ; sometimes nobody knows, or nobody says ! What tribe ? Check the position. Reload the camera, whose film I must arrange to have finished (no time yet to repair that of the caid). Note-book ; foot. Quinine. Tea. Food (for two days I have eaten nothing, it is true, on account of fever, except a little barley at about ten o'clock—not very good).

Departures are always sudden, after the fashion of caravanners. A sheikh calls ' Ahmed ! ' (Ahmed is asleep, or eating.)

Ahmed : ' *Naam ?* ' (What).

He must stir himself at once, and there is hardly

[1] The author means the compass, whose needle ' see-saws ' to the Arab mind.

time to get to the camel, in the midst of a gargle, before it is loaded. Then I must hoist myself into the saddle, and beware of the pitching backwards and forwards as the beast rises, unless I am to be thrown head first to the earth.

Same halt. 3.45.

El Mahboul has just told me that of the 30,000 francs, the sheikh of Tigilit has given 10,000 francs to the Reguibat and Aït Chogout sheikhs : and is to give them a similar amount on the return to Tigilit : will give, or has given, several thousands to a second Reguibat (against the possibility of my falling prisoner, in which event this sheikh has undertaken to reclaim me and take me back to Tigilit), and odd amounts to Chibani, Ali, and Lhassen.

The Reguibat sheikh (one of my two guides) demanded a million, it appears.

Same halt. 6 *o'clock.*

We are held up. The sick sheikh refuses to go farther. Ill ; foot bad ; a thorn. They even want to go back to Tigilit. The Reguibat sheikh is a dirty blackguard. He would do this to annoy me. They seem to have decided to stay here, or in the vicinity of water, until the Aït Chogout sheikh gets better.

That individual has redoubled his prayers. I was going to take his pulse, but while I was a few inches away he pulled back his hand, and began his invocations in a loud voice, performed his ceremonial ablutions with a stone, and even prostrated himself, in spite of his foot.

Wednesday, October 8.   Same halt, 7 a.m.

Last night El Mahboul gave me to understand that the sheikhs have made up their minds to return to Tigilit on account of the foot of the Aït Chogout.

For a long time I could not sleep.

The Reguibat sheikh passing by, I told him again, with some force, that the troubles of his companion were not serious, &c. After that conversation, he seems to have made up his mind to stay in some place where there is water, until the Aït Chogout is better.

10 o'clock halt.

The sheikhs refused to go on to Smara. They want to pose as traders, and propose to buy sugar at Tigilit or in some souk more to the north, and start again with more camels and more men.

I refused, refused, refused.

I shall try to clean up the sheikh's foot, make him wait for a day, and then move on towards Smara.

Not very cheerful.

From eight o'clock till ten o'clock we retraced our steps, along the way we came yesterday. [At nine o'clock] we stopped near water. [The sheikhs refilled the water-skins and went on again.

It was obvious that they were taking the way back to Tigilit. I made my camel kneel. El Mahboul threw his stick to the ground, tore off his turban. For a moment, I had the idea of letting the sheikhs go on to the north, and of continuing south with El Mahboul, taking a course by the compass, and trying to get into touch with a native.

But it was on the cards that I should not have one chance in a thousand of succeeding. I let this idea

go, very quickly, and, with night in my heart, followed
the sheikhs.]

We continued for another hour and came to a stop.
Here, at ten o'clock. El Mahboul is very good.

Same halt. 2.30.

For an hour, bathed the foot of the Aït Chogout
sheikh in a saucepanful of (muddy) water, in which
I dissolved six tablets of clonazone. Also gave him
three aspirin tablets. At this moment, I, myself,
am on my back, with my right foot in the saucepan.

Thursday, October 9.

Yesterday, tried every means to persuade the sheikh :
promised him a revolver, money—he will not see
Tiznit—Jean would give him soporifics, &c.

' No, no ! Tigilit, not Smara.'

What was there to do ? Go back, and start again
with four camels, sugar, two men, four water-skins—
one of our two, punctured, was repaired with clay, and
continues to leak.

Provided that the cost is the same. . . .

Provided that the sheikh's foot does not become
poisoned. . . .

At half-past six, while I ate a little maize near the
fire, the Reguibat sheikh went to look for the camels
in the bushes.

Suddenly : two dull shots, then another, and the
whistle of bullets over our heads. Direction : from
the south. The Arabs put the firing at about two
miles. I, a little nearer, remembering the ranges at
Mazagan. Better to be gone out of it. Flight. The
baroud. Compulsion.

VIEW OF THE VALLEY WHERE THE FIRST ATTEMPT WAS INTERRUPTED
OCTOBER 7, MORNING

SAME VALLEY.   ACACIAS
OCTOBER 7, MORNING

Baggage. One water-skin empty, the other half full. The hot water in the *mokraj*, put on the fire for tea, and which El Mahboul was about to throw away, poured back into the skin. Splendid fight between the Reguibat sheikh and the young camel when he wanted to tie the muzzle (so that the camel could not begin screaming, and give away our position). The sheikh threw himself into the saddle, and the camel turned itself over on its side (my bag on the pommel !) ; but the sheikh kept his hold, while the other sheikh fixed the thong. A few low cries, then, little by little they faded into silence. Darkness, and later, the moon behind the crests of the hills.

Before mounting the camel, the Aït Chogout sheikh instructed me by signs :

' If the Arabs surprise us and come shouting round us, don't stop. Drive your camel this way and that, to right and left, and fly.'

I mounted. He rode on the cruppers of his beast, crouching behind the saddle, stuck like a louse to his mount, fearing another volley. I, with my white djellaba, perched high, came last of the group. El Mahboul pulled my camel along with the cord round its muzzle (while I beat a tattoo on its rump).

Every eye hunted here and there. Men ?

Nobody knew where they might be.

The narrow valley, with its rocks and bushes, not all travelling at the same speed. The full moon throwing light and shade. The summits here and there with crags that looked like men. They could be seen to move !

Sometimes I hunched my back, anticipating a bullet. My satchel slung across my shoulders, resting on my

stomach. But what was the use ? I did not know
where the enemy was. Believe me, I made my act of
contrition. It would have been very easy to end there.
I had none of the fever of the other three.

At the blind end of the valley, the Reguibat sheikh,
who was hurrying along, perhaps thirty yards from
us, stopped and listened. When we caught up with
him, he showed us the bushes to the left. I listened
and, as I looked, made out a white shape. Suddenly
it moved, going before us at about fifty yards, and
passed to our right with a galloping sound. Was it
a horse, whose rider had been killed ? A moufflon
(white moufflon ?).

' A man,' said El Mahboul.

But a man does not run like that.

The noise gone, we resumed our march. Relatively
easy climb out of the valley. What a sigh of relief
when there were no more rocks, bushes, crests, those
sudden shadows ; but only rolling country, and, later,
the plain.

I believed we were out of danger when cries pierced
the darkness to our right : a man, perhaps seven or
eight hundred yards away. Then, silence again.
We did not slow down.

[The road we followed lay slightly to the east of our
outward track, and carried us along a rise in the
earth, not very marked—90 feet ?]

The sheikh said that we should have to cross a
desert plain, and probably be two days without water.
Stopped El Mahboul, who was about to take a drink.

Vegetation grew sparse, but there were still bushes
in clumps. Crossing one of these spots, El Mahboul,
who was leading my camel by its nose, jumped from

ONE OF THE POINTS OF WATER
ENCOUNTERED DURING THE MORNING OF OCTOBER 7

SAME POINT OF WATER
OCTOBER 8, AT 9 A.M.

right to left. At the same time I heard a hiss ; or rather, something like a cylinder of oxygen or liquid air with the tap open, and I saw an enormous snake, as thick as my arm and nearly six feet long, ready to strike.

When we had reached bare earth, I could no longer hold back my laughter at the thought of the antics of El Mahboul ; and El Mahboul laughed with me, but perhaps on the other side of his face.

Turning round in my saddle, I looked behind us very often.

The vegetation thinned and disappeared. The earth : hard sand. The horizon made the circle of the compass. A perfect disc.

Stopped. The sheikhs adjusted the camel-loads. A seat was improvised behind each saddle. I rode behind the Aït Chogout sheikh, El Mahboul behind the Reguibat. It became nothing less than a flight. The Reguibat sheikh, fearful that they would pick up our tracks and give chase, constantly looked behind.

So until three o'clock. Unspeakable fatigue : the small of my back, my buttocks pounded to death. My foot, which hung heavily, swollen, painful, as though it were ready to drop off my leg. Riding astride the enormous beast threatened to split me open : the hard backbone, ropes, only a djellaba to ride on. Gun on the knees, a switch for the camel's rump. Could not think. But, by flashes, as though deluded by that disc, a vision of the earth. The sun, setting with us, would shine on Melbourne, Australia, Sydney, the Pacific. Steamers under way ; people awake in their state-rooms ; the houses, restaurants, streets, dances.

Soon, I should see the sun again, and they begin their night.

At three o'clock, a halt. Very soft sand. Calm after the storm. Even the worst experiences pass. Rest ; well-being. (The Reguibat sheikh, who begins to have a little confidence in me, asked where the shots came from, if I saw the men ; he, who, a little while ago, while he was rounding up the camels, saw, or believed he saw, a man and a camel in the dim twilight.)

Roused at five o'clock. My place still on the cruppers. Weariness which had to be fought from moment to moment. Took a photograph, just the same, but the release came adrift. I began all over again.

To hang on, I bit my lower lip—nearly down to the chin. Bruised, feverish.

I saw the lone mountain which we passed on the way out.

Halt finally at the same place where we camped on Sunday [named Amezera]. In the dead embers of the fire, El Mahboul found some silver paper which had been wrapped round my chocolate.

What weariness ! But El Mahboul came to tell me that we were to continue at once, and on we went.

So much effort for nothing. Everything to be begun afresh.

Friday, October 10.   6 *o'clock halt.*
Yesterday at half-past eleven, we resumed our journey. The plain ended, we attacked the slopes of

the djebel Ouargziz (three or four miles). I do not know why I should find this stretch so full of foreboding. Before [on the outward journey], how I protested against the Tree.

This time : noon, overhead sun on my back, lameness which prevented my breathing, riveted to the saddle. I saw a grotesque shadow : a priest with biretta above, tail and the huge legs of a beast below ; disagreeable vision—or perhaps it was only the earth, the stony miles travelled in reverse (no longer towards Smara) which will now have to be done again.

Finally, on the top, I dismounted. I turned to look back, and saw, as clearly as an aviator, land which I knew. I saw the long road we had travelled, the parallel ranges.

The pleasure of recognition. The Ouargziz, which stretched out to the east and west. There are only two passes, El Mahboul tells me ; one here, the other farther to the east. An abrupt slope ; wonderful view. All the bed of the Ouargziz : valleys to the west which are not on my route, to the east the two roads which lead to Tigilit. Everything stood out clearly [no photograph : camera on the camel].

Descent not too tiring. Road better for travel than the first time, because of the sick sheikh (the other time we went by the rocks). The camels ahead, myself hobbling along behind with the sheikh. However, at the end, El Mahboul helped me. The sick sheikh was hoisted on to a camel, and went off ahead with the Reguibat sheikh. They did not stop until they had gone a full mile into the plain. I was furious. I climbed down little by little with El Mahboul, reaching the bottom about half-past three.

By way of apology, the Reguibat sheikh surrendered his place in the saddle to me, and walked.

According to El Mahboul, the valley is tilled when there is no baroud. We found the water-hole, the tombs and the marabout again.

At six o'clock, a few minutes' halt. Sunset. El Mahboul kept watch from a rock. Prayers.

This time, when we started again, I rode on the cruppers behind the Aït Chogout sheikh. Very dark night. My loins. Legs ! The camel often in the thorns : my legs. Always listening intently, scanning everything in sight.

About eight o'clock : rest. Fine sand. Awoke at three o'clock. Then the sheikh lay down again. Another hour's sleep. Hard waking. I thought of the number of days, of the hardship.

Riding behind the Aït Chogout sheikh, he taught me his prayers. The other suggested that I should go home with him and he would give me a wife : ' *Mezian, mezian.*' [1] I told him that I had a wife already, but thanked him just the same.

At six o'clock, halt. Tea, barley. As I write, the Reguibat sheikh and El Mahboul are gathering wood and stones. Two camp-fires—barley, arganier. Some one calls me.

[12.30 *halt.   Oued Dra.*]

We followed a road, or rather some terribly difficult mountains where we were almost certain to meet nobody. (I should have liked to take a photograph.) The Reguibat sheikh went ahead. I rode one camel

[1] ' Very beautiful.'

and the Aït Chogout sheikh the other, with precipices of three hundred feet or more below us, and where it would have been dangerous to falter ; so steep that I ceased to ride astride on the cruppers like the sheikh, and clung to the saddle. But sometimes, although they are very sure-footed, the camels stumbled and narrowly escaped a fall. If they fell : precipice. I was finally compelled to walk.

On top. Almost perpendicular descent, made on foot (my two bruised feet). Heavy black rocks, with marks like screws, encrusted with shells. Rocks so high that El Mahboul had to take me in his arms.

We called from above to the sheikh below.

The ear : the sound came from everywhere, from all the valley. An ordinary voice : I heard it, but it was unintelligible.

The eye : details that were not fixed, I could not see ; fixed, I could recognize them, and spell them out.

Below : very broken. I rode the she-camel, big with her young, and after following a road that was relatively good, and later very good, we reached the Oued Dra. Water. Halt at half-past twelve. Drank more than half a saucepanful.

Only one thing brings any happiness to me. To-night I shall find letters from Jean, from Jeannie—from mother, perhaps—things they have sent me, tins of fruit, &c., I shall stay five or six days at Tigilit, or even seven, to give myself necessary treatment, to recuperate. I know now that I can cover 110 to 120 miles in forty-eight hours, going day and night, by camel and on foot, and that not on French roads, but often among stiff mountainous country (you should have seen the camels in the mountains). Those

overturned boulders, the dreadful irregularities, seen
from above. That is all one looks at : the hollows, the
ridges. They give a staggering idea of terrestrial
formations.

My back can stand it. My legs, my feet, I hope, will
be healed. I hope also that all will be well with the
sheikhs. And in six days we shall start again, and this
time come through successfully, I think.

Where we are now are water ; green grass ; birds ;
rushes ; trees.

During these seven days, not a man : some tombs.

6 *p.m. halt.*

We have been on the march since three o'clock. We
shall reach Tigilit about 2 a.m., our route completely
retraced. I recognized the place where we ate last
Saturday.

.   .   .   .

At first I rode behind the Aït Chogout sheikh, then
on the young mehari ; almost comfortable, even at
ease. The Aït Chogout sheikh is unwearying. He
rehearses his prayers to me.

I was hardly able to use the compass. At first I
concentrated on the journey, but later I discovered
that, as we were not following the good road, by way
of the principal valleys and passes, but were keeping
among the secondary ranges and making constant
detours, the compass was almost a source of error. I
did use it, but only a little. On the heights there was
much to see, to take in. A compass, without compre-
hension, is labour in vain, I fear. On the heights :
orientation, photographs, and observation. There-
after, an effort to understand where one is, without

giving too much importance to the immediate locality. I shall put that to use.

Here, at the foot of a valley, in a very strange clump of mountains, we have come to rest. Almost night. There is a brushwood fire. Tea, barley, with a little onion.

El Mahboul goes apart from time to time, to listen for sounds in the dark.

I V

BACK AT TIGILIT

Tigilit ! Saturday. 3.15 *a.m.*
Back again. In the house belonging to Lhassen. Saw
Muhammed. No letters yet, because Lhassen is here.

* * *

Our way retraced during the night. The Reguibat
sheikh said to me :
' If they come shouting round you, recite, " *Ashhadou
anna la ilaha ill' Allah. Ashhadou anna Muhammed
Rassoul Allah,*" ' and went on ahead.
We came upon him again suddenly, on the brow of
a hill—scouting the way. Hard going. Neither man
nor beast could do more. Even the sheikhs were
holding their backs.
The beginning, however, was quite easy, very agreeable, on the big she-camel which El Mahboul led by the
nose, through a valley where the roads were good. I
thought of how good Smara will be, how it will repay
us for everything if we are ultimately successful ; how
it will give significance to our lives, to our gestures ; of
how I am going to keep myself at it till I succeed ; of
my life with these nomads who are not used to living
in houses : worlds apart from the things of civilized
Europe—their religions : one, so threadbare although
full of pomp ; the other, ceremonies, &c.

Then we were among jagged mountains, alone on my camel, hanging on behind the saddle, arms nearly powerless, the jumps which almost tore me from the saddle shaped like a cup, with high back and pommel, and only the void below. Before this descent—a long prayer by the sheikhs ; no doubt a prayer of thanks to Allah.

6.45.

Have not been able to sleep. Too weary. Too many flies. And then, your news,[1] news of Jeannie which you tell me. Under the candle, I was there, cooped up for an hour, wanting to hide that from the Arabs.

I have not re-read what I wrote last night, but I know that it is not brilliant : weariness, like poverty, saps the mind.

After the mountain, hillocks to cross. This time with the Reguibat sheikh in the saddle. I did not know where to sit, to prevent lurching about, to avoid falling.

Before reaching Tigilit, we met a man. We came to a halt at a distance of about fifty yards, facing each other, the sheikhs gun in hand. We stared at each other. We passed by, the man slipped into the bushes.

About two o'clock, we reached Tigilit locked in its hills, whose sides are curiously worked in serpentine twists. I was left lying down about five hundred yards

[1] My brother knew that I should be the first to read these notes, which would be delivered to me at Mogador by our messengers.

from the town with El Mahboul while the sheikhs went to the sheikh of Tigilit. Slept. Roused an hour later by Lhassen. Covered the five hundred yards of pebbles and stones painfully on foot. Rising alleys. Lhassen's house. As soon as he went, the letters.

* * *

All that work . . . Smara not reached, because of a single thorn.

* * *

The journey showed what we grasp of the earth : so many valleys, so many rocks—of its magnitude that has no common measure with mankind.

* * *

If we travel over the same ground again, I shall make an itinerary and topographical survey (with photographs)—very good, I think. Otherwise, I shall survey another route. Less and less of the picturesque, more of what is useful. Such-and-such a hill, road, or pass.

It must be said that El Mahboul has been splendid, and put up a magnificent show.

* * *

To-day I must write to Jean, Jeannie, Father, Garachon, &c., dress my feet, take a look at the medicine-chest, and make up packets.

* * *

I have just eaten some goat, barley cakes, and dates with real appetite ! It heartens me to see the way in which the body revives. Last night I opened a tin of cherries (the others for Smara). They were gulped

RECTILINEAR CREST OF DJEBEL OUARGZIZ, SEEN FROM AMEZERA
OCTOBER 9, 9.30 A.M.

SOUTHERN FLANK OF DJEBEL OUARGZIZ
ABOUT MIDDAY, OCTOBER 10

down in a few minutes with El Mahboul, but I had
at least three-quarters myself. What a welcome
relief this kindly food is to a stomach that has been
jolted about for days.

Only one thing worries me now. Shall we get away
quickly? Will there be some new impediment? These
Arabs change their minds so quickly : the sheikhs ;
sometimes agreeable ; sometimes surly. (I think I
did not relate how, during the descent of the Ouargziz,
they went off down the valley for about a mile, perhaps,
leaving me there with my lame foot—confidence in
El Mahboul.)

Have I mentioned the sheikh's foot? Still swollen.
At the Ouargziz, having tapped his foot, he complained
that there was no feeling in his toes, except in the big toe
and in part of the instep. I was afraid myself, it must
be admitted—the swelling, the flesh without any
elasticity : gangrene? But a thorn. . . . He could
run. There was nothing the matter. It seems to me
that it is not so serious, and even if it were it would be
imperative for us to go on to Smara (but he is almost
indispensable, because he is the only one with relatives
down there), and to summon Jean here, on conditions
that . . . that . . .
How thoroughly I debated the question in my mind !

(Did I make a note of the fact that the reason the
sheikh of Tigilit chose a Reguibat and an Aït Chogout
was so that we should have friends everywhere?
Because here, both the Reguibat and the Aït Chogout

are in danger, just as I am, or is Chibani.   At Smara
itself, our protector will be the Aït Chogout.)

* * *

I may not have mentioned this.   We travelled
during some of the nights with El Mahboul leading
the Aït Chogout sheikh by the hand.

* * *

The bowl, full of maize, on which rests a fine piece
of moufflon for the women.   They invite me to par-
ticipate.   I take a lot of it.

* * *

The Aït Chogout sheikh has just climbed up here
to make a call.   I looked at his foot, which seems to
be getting better.   Seated around a basketful of dates,
Chibani, El Mahboul, Muhammed.   And the interminable arguments began again.   The Aït Chogout
proposed going first to Smara, to mark out the parts
where we may expect danger.   El Mahboul said,
' No !   Smara at once ! '

Otherwise I shall still be here after a hundred days
have elapsed.

Sunday, October 12.

Spent the day writing to Jean, Jeannie, parents,
Garachon, and going over the bearings of my itinerary
as well as could be, &c.

Monday, October 13.

Muhammed still here.   He ought to leave for
Goulimin at the same time as the Reguibat sheikh,
to buy two meharis and sugar.   The people of

Goulimin having stolen all the beasts that belonged
to the people of Tigilit, these latter are compelled to
go to Goulimin and buy them back. But when are
Muhammed and the Reguibat sheikh going to make
a start ?

Now, it is not to Goulimin that they are going for
the camels, but to a souk that is being held beyond
El Akhsas. (Sidi Bou Abeli. The fair lasts for three
days—9000 men.) And it needs three days for the
journey there. We shall not get away in less than seven
days !

* * *

I have recopied my itinerary, correcting certain
details.

* * *

Muhammed left at 4.30,[1] and I shall still be here for
six full days.

[1] On October 20, Muhammed arrived at Mogador and delivered to me the letter from my brother :

'TIGILIT, *Saturday, October* 11, *2 o'clock.*

' MY DEAR JEAN,—I am terribly sorry to disappoint you. I
shall not be at the Oued Massa by the 17th. We only left during
the night of 3rd/4th, and I have been forced to come back to
Tigilit, the first attempt having failed—under conditions that you
will see. I can assure you that I did my utmost to persuade the
sheikhs to go forward.

. . . .

' To put it briefly, to-day I ought to be at Smara, but it has
all to be started over again.

' I am still apprehensive of difficulties. I have seen the mis-
trust of the sheikhs. But there is no difficulty that I shall not
try to overcome.

' In fact, I think that everything will go well. There will be

Tuesday, October 14.

In this room, six feet wide and about twenty-four
to thirty feet long, with a door at one end about three

more of us. We shall have sugar to sell. (Never forget, whatever
happens, that I pass for an American trader.)

' One thing has helped me to return, the thought that I should
have news of you. I am going to rest here and give my feet the
treatment they need, and I know that once Smara is reached, I
shall not be so sorry that the first effort failed. It has enabled me
to survey one route, and it seems likely, because the baroud is so
continual in the country that we are to cross, that we shall take
another road. The baroud is the only danger that I run (because, taken prisoner, I am fairly sure that I should soon be released). The baroud is regularly met with here, but you should
have seen the precautions, the changes of route, that the sheikhs
took. And then, the baroud is generally directed against the
people who are in charge of flocks and herds.

' I hope to leave Tigilit in six or seven days. Seven days must
be allowed for the outward journey and seven for the return ; two
there. The road can be covered in four days, going day and
night (as we did on Thursday and Friday) ; but that would not be
so useful for me : almost no photographs, a dull mind at the halts,
feet which really can stand no more. At present, six sores, not
too big, and a swollen ankle. I wash in clonazone, and I think
that, without being entirely healed, in four or five days I shall be
able to walk. To-day, I can only drag myself along . . . and
my back !

.   .   .   .

' But it was necessary to tell you that. What peace, what
security, to feel myself helped along in such a way. With you I
can do anything.

' *Monday, October* 13.

' More delay. They are not going to Goulimin for the camels,
but beyond El Akhsas, to a souk that is now being held. They
will need three days for the return : I shall not leave Smara for
another week. Find out from Muhammed if they were able to get
—the 16th or 17th at the latest—what they went for (some good

feet high, from which one descends by the stairs to
the courtyard—the only opening, unless I count the
two loopholes, which, incidentally, do give me a view
over the oued, the mountains, the sheikh's house, and
the tents. The nearest tent, I discovered yesterday,
is that of the harlots : three women who spend their
days hunting lice, and, when they have visitors, as
they did yesterday, clap their hands and sing, talking
all night while they carry on their love-making.

Two people have just come to this room that I
occupy, to call on me—on me, and the tea (we have
no more sugar), and on the goat's meat : the Aït
Chogout still limping, and Lhassen's wife with her
little daughter, three years old, perhaps, with sore eyes
that have been eaten by the flies. This youngster,
when she opens her mouth to say ' Mama ' like a little

camels). In that case, keep in mind the following dates : 19th
or 20th : start. 25th or 26th : Smara. Leave Smara the 27th.
At Tigilit on the 1st. Oued Massa by the 7th or 8th.

. . . . . .
' My feet will have healed in seven days. That is one thing to
the good. I shall be able to walk, and not simply drag along.
' 2 o'clock.
' El Mahboul asks for another five thousand francs for the
purchase of camels, sugar, &c. What is there to do ? We must
get there. But it disgusts me, asking for so much money and not
to be at Smara yet.

. . . . . .
' P.S.—We shall not start till the night of Sunday/Monday.'
* * *
My brother also acknowledged the receipt of the money and
the things I had sent him. He asked for preserved fruits, ham,
films, and sundry medicines.

With the letters, my brother gave the notes and photographs
already taken to Muhammed.

I sent Muhammed back to Tigilit on October 23.

French child, has the only voice, the only language which is anything like that of my own country. And it is so long since I heard anything but Chleuh and the few twisted words of El Mahboul.

I talked to the Aït Chogout, to keep him well-disposed to us : telling him that I am going to ship sugar, clothes, &c., by sea, that Tigilit will be one of my branches, &c. (Tigilit is, it seems, only a day's journey from the sea.)

* * *

The raid, and particularly the last two days, stays in my mind like a dream. I remember it as an unfolding reel of film of the enclosed valley and the djebel.

I had a sort of intoxication—of weariness.

Flashes of memory : on the beast, attacked by the sun, fatigue ; that ego contented, erect, showing its mettle, breathing the very essence of action, purified by its very flame, feeling itself of the elect, at the very core. How good it is, what strength it gives ! The head bursts with joy, in spite of suffering, lameness, sun, and thirst.

This recurs like a chorus :

This thing that we have purposed, we shall do. We are moving towards the goal, armed by all the days of our waiting, by everything that has worked in us since our birth.

To-day, joy ; expanding, flowering under my feet. I feel myself ready for everything, and, as my witnesses . . .

Wednesday, October 15.

This morning, at the first hint of dawn, Chibani, who sleeps in the courtyard, mounted to my floor with

a sugar-loaf under his arm and, before the Arabs
began to move about, made, with what infinite care,
the tea of which we ought to be deprived until Sunday.

El Mahboul, who has seen the sheikh, told me that
he wants us to leave Tigilit at once, with Chibani,
because Merebbi Rebbo, who is making his annual
tour with an escort of three hundred men, is in these
parts. Nobody knows whether he will come to Tigilit
or move straight on to the Oued Noun. El Mahboul
suggested that if he is likely to pass this way (which
the sheikh will learn from his scouts) we should leave
with Chibani, and the sheikhs could rejoin us at the
Oued Dra, for instance, where we could wait for them.
Merebbi Rebbo would stay about three days at
Tigilit, during which (this is my idea) men of his escort
might probably be lodged in this house.

Questioned El Mahboul about Merebbi Rebbo.
His influence hardly extends beyond the Dra. He has,
so to speak, no authority at all over the Reguibat,
Izargiin, &c., who refuse to pay him tribute. He has
power over the country of the Oued Noun : Goulimin,
&c.

At Smara, sometimes there are 1000 men, sometimes
500, sometimes 100 : some telamid,[1] some Reguibat,
some Aït Youssa. A few houses, two good citadels,
the house of Ma el Aïnin, in ruins. Many palm-trees.

I should like to use this forced stay to visit the djebel,
and photograph Tigilit—but what if I ruin my feet ?
I do not know what I shall do.

[1] Disciples (of Ma el Aïnin).

Flies, in their thousands.

An ache in my ankle. The sores seem to be healing a little.

3 o'clock.

Rested for an hour on the hard mat, one foot in the basin (four tablets to a quart of water). Even though I have only about twenty left, I decided on this extra bathing, there being some inflammation round the sores and feeling shooting pains in my ankle.

Lice once again. And, since yesterday, enteritis. A little my own fault : ate too much. I must watch myself.

I hardly know how to describe the strange relief I experience : caring for my feet, counting my medicines, mending my rags, eating barley, checking my appetite for dates, the delay of some days ; everything seems to work together to further this effort, the first since our birth, piling high our hopes, opening up to us other roads than those already travelled, and which, at any price, we intend to explore.

It is hard to wait here, just the same, the more so because the goal is yet to be reached. But I do not find the days entirely without interest, although they are boring, because sometimes the fever of longing, the sense of something lost now recovered, makes me lose all thought of the hardness of the earth, of lice, feet, and long idle hours, and carries me into its golden circle.

How sad it must be never, never to touch the apples of the Hesperides, of which, as children or men, we catch a glimpse, or perhaps caress, but which, for all that, remain in the gardens of illusion.

Oh ! lovely orchard into which we have entered, body and soul.

When I think of the burial of Bagnolet, I find all death glorious. Could a closer, more intense communion exist anywhere than that which unites us ? I feel that I am not alone.

5.30.
From a loophole. On the flat roof of the nearest house, dates of many colours in heaps : one yellow, one almost black, one ruddy, one brown, and bunches on fine fronds of golden yellow. And a man, dressed in blue robes—a vigorous old fellow, bald and bareheaded—who slowly stoops and rises, goes from one heap to another, samples them, throws the stones away. The only man in this corner of a country of palms girdled by mountains.

I cannot say what lent grandeur to the scene : the time ? The absence of sun, after a day of intense heat and brilliant light ?

Outside, not a sound save the occasional bleating of goats—hair-raising prattle of Bous and Ahmed ; their northern costumes seem to me something of a profanation.

(It is dark : I can no longer see what I write.)

Written at night.
It is not a wide horizon that I see ; cut off to right and left by the narrowness of the loophole, in front by the near mountain. If I lie flat on the mat, I can see the sky and the outline of the crests.

A little below, two or three flat roofs ; and the earth sloping away to the nearby oued, with its dark verdure of palm-trees, and which itself follows the foot of the mountain.

Women and children, who stream silently on to the roofs.

In the evening, the courtyard is full of bleating.

The other night I awoke, noise very near to me ; a goat which had clambered up. Was she making a meal of my papers ? (Montherlant.) No ! Chased off.

Thursday, October 16.

Last night, when I had gone to bed and was nearly asleep, there was a grand gala in one of the houses of Tigilit : recitations (in the manner of the litanies of the clergy), rifle shots, &c.

That prompted Lhassen's wife to give us a party also. She summoned men and women. I left my place and lay flat in front of the door, beside El Mahboul.

The women gathered slowly. Their silhouettes in the shadows of the court. Twenty women and ten men, or thereabouts. And, on the roofs all round the courtyard, a dozen silhouettes rose to watch the show. The women were grouped in a corner and accompanied themselves by clapping their hands and feet in rhythm, as they began one of their simple songs, seeking unison. They recited, interpolated by ' Io ! Io ! ' half a dozen of these songs, each one having the same rhythm, from beginning to end. Only the words changed, and that very gradually. I shall try to pick up the words, and even the rhythm.

The negro, our neighbour of the lower story, took his old *mok'hala* and let off half a dozen shots, to mark the high spots of the festival. As the shots were fired, the cries of ' Io ! Io ! ' became more intense.

I stayed so for about half an hour, then, as the fête still continued (just as questions and answers were being made by both men and women), I stretched myself out again on my marabout's cloak.

Little by little the merry-making died down. The people left, laughing and talking together, and I . . . went to sleep.

Noon.

Blinding sun outside. Here, body streaming wet. Clouds of flies. One covers up, and cannot breathe.

And I think of what they told me : too much sun : route practically impassible to Smara, not a drop of water. On the other hand, if it rains, the Dra unfordable for seven or eight days.

Did I mention that they buy and sell water here ?

Redissolved a few drops of tincture of iodine in mint-alcohol. I had put the solid residue on one side. Everything evaporates, with only corks as seals ; they do not close any more, too dry, do not hold in the necks of the bottles.

Written by the light of the four-nosed oil-lamp . . . shaped like an antique.

Ali's brother-in-law was killed (I mentioned the fact ten or twelve days ago) while pasturing our ass. He had asked ten francs for the job.

Chibani is the former sheikh of this place. Left Tigilit for Tamanar because the baroud never left him in peace.[1]

Drank a bowl of goats' milk with a barley cake : the first time I have had both together.

Berated El Mahboul because, under the pretext that he wanted to enjoy the company of some woman or other, he made me go into that half of the room that is infested by lice.

The furniture here : the small wooden tray on which they put the glasses for the tea ; or the copper tray. The large wooden dish for couscous,[2] repaired with a metal plate.

Friday, October 17.

Poor Jean, two or three bad days to get through until you receive my letters and notes.

* * *

Night almost more insufferable than the day. This fearfully hard earth. I do not know where to put my feet, my back, my shoulder. Oh ! if I could only have those nights in the sand. I sleep for ten minutes and the painful contact of the thin mat wakens me, forces me to change my position.

---

[1] The caid Haddou, in December 1930, confirmed to me that Chibani had been a sheikh of Tigilit fifteen years previously, and that he had had to leave the district, because, at the instigation of the Aït Oussa, he had organized an ambush in which twelve Aït Messoud, his guests, were killed. Chibani, so that he might enter Tigilit on September 20, 1930, and return in good favour, made his peace with the sheikh of Tigilit.

[2] Native hash.

In the morning, while the day has scarcely broken, almost before sunrise : the flies, which wake in swarms and begin their buzzing.

To-day, nothing to eat but barley, No more sugar, no more goat-flesh. I was forgetting the dates. But, since they are uncooked, if I eat them I risk finding myself feverish again. I eat as few of them as possible, which is to say : a lot.

* * *

Sad discovery I made this morning : at the bottom of the tin tube in which the tablets of clonazone are kept, I saw something white, and thought it was tablets that the jolts had reduced to powder : it was only cotton-wool. There are only nine tablets left.

* * *

Have I recorded this conversation between the sheikhs, El Mahboul and myself, during the first raid ?

'. . . If we find ourselves in a neighbourhood where many people are travelling, are you agreeable to travel in a sack, like sugar ? '

'. . . Yes, if it is only for a little while.'

10 *o'clock.*

Once we have made Smara, our youth will be completed. I feel it. We shall enter on another period.

* * *

It should be possible to say what you are to me at these times.[1] Our twin souls : our wills ; and in my body it is almost as though a ligament bound me to you.

. . . .

[1] Cf. note, p. 135.

Lhassen's wife and her little daughter here. The ease with which the woman carries her child (by one arm, on her back), and with which she goes through the low doorway.

* * *

My feet ! Shall I still have to drag myself on my knees to the camel ?

Saturday, October 18. 8 *a.m.*

It is almost decided that we shall take a route west of the one taken the last time.   Impossible to check up my previous itinerary. But, on the other hand, I shall see another section of the Sahara.

* * *

Perhaps I had better make a note of this.

Last night, having already gone to bed (this oasis of the Dra is gay with festivals every evening), El Mahboul, coming from the sheikh, told me that :

1. The people of El Bordj accuse Chibani of having introduced a ' roumi ' into the country and have put it to the sheikh of Tigilit, who has denied it.

2. To keep the sheikhs in hand, El Mahboul was obliged to say, ' M. Jean (brother Mr. Vieuchange) will come here.   How much ? '

' A million,' says the Aït Chogout.

' Not fifty thousand ?   Not one hundred thousand ? '

' No, two hundred thousand,' says the Aït Chogout.

' No ! one hundred thousand.'

Moreover, the sheikh of Tigilit asked for the immediate payment of the remainder of the thirty thousand.

I felt myself hemmed in. A sort of fever. Up to then I had been so calm always. I asked myself :

'Am I going to be ill?' And I said to myself that I was only a quarter of the way on my journey. That troubled me, bothered me. These men at my heels. I mean a fortune to them. Should they get wind that I am a European, there would be more than a thousand to hunt us through the Sahara, and the Reguibat and Aït Chogout sheikhs none too reliable. The sheikh of Tigilit is dependable, it seems.

This morning, perfectly self-possessed.

10 *o'clock.*

Chibani has killed a goat. How much that is going to cost me, I don't know.

We have to hide the meat ; otherwise, we should be invaded by all the inhabitants of the oasis.

The Aït Chogout appeared at once, hardly limping at all. I had not seen him for several days . . . but the meat !

He has shaved his head like Ahmed, with my razor. Have I sketched his portrait before this operation? Hair black as ink ; coarse features ; thick lips ; puffy swellings and wrinkles coming down from the sides of his nose ; a rather shaggy beard ; sore eyes, bloodshot.

Noon.

The Aït Chogout tried to persuade me that Chibani ought not to accompany us to Smara : wounded heel, getting old, no stomach, &c.

After that argument, I was almost sure that if Chibani did not come with us these two sheikhs would play us a dirty trick : there was every chance of being taken captive ; or, at every twenty miles ' How much

will you give us to go farther ? '   And would they go
all the way to Smara ?

I shall not go without Chibani.

* * *

I asked Lhassen's wife to tell me the words of her
songs. I wrote them out. But—the gestures and
intonations . . .

3.30.

Have I spoken of this especial pleasure at the halts :
making my notes, checking my instruments, and
round me these cross-grained quibblers getting ready
something to eat, with El Mahboul—who is faithful—
helping them, hunting for wood. All that to make
possible something we were determined upon.

Sunday, October 19.   10.30.

It ought to be after nightfall to-day that we make
a start. I think only of that. But the Reguibat
sheikh has not yet returned.

* * *

Thou bearest us on thy mighty wings.   Thy strength
sufficeth for two.

Because of thee, all fears and all anguish are banished.
In the imagination of youth, ofttimes they range themselves before us. If I look to the right or to the left,
I am like unto them : their voice is as mine, and I
know the narrow limits of my intelligence.

Yet do I also feel the leaven that worketh in me.

Words, that plough your brain.

The first proofs, while yet bountiful, were incomplete.

But thou removest us far from uncertainty and doubt, far from perplexity, and from the days of idle thought that cause the spirit to waver. So cast down that a man sees only his little circle—as any other—and asks no more than to be allowed to remain as he is. The arm-chair and indolence alone are esteemed. But thou, thou carriest us away on thy mighty wings.

* * *

Dreary waiting hours, almost insufferable.

2.30.

The Reguibat sheikh still not returned from the souk. Uncomfortable hours to get through. Is it this anxiety that has given me this headache ?

5 *o'clock*.

Still nobody.

Monday, October 20. 6 *a.m.*

Still at Tigilit, and neither the sheikh, nor Lhassen, nor Ali, nor the camels, nor the sugar, has arrived from the souk. It cannot be the baroud, apparently, because there are too many men on the roads.

It seems that when Chibani and Muhammed were coming back from Tiznit they were seen by the inhabitants of Fask or Tagant, and that ten men waited for them on the road we took from El Bordj here. But Chibani, scenting an ambush, took another route.

7 *o'clock*.

Chibani has discovered a little Spanish sugar in the house of one of the people of Tigilit, promising to return the same quantity on the arrival of the camels. For the last half hour we have all been gathered round the tray (with Lhassen's wife and her little daughter Taboucat) while Bous makes the tea. I take in all the significance of this drink, the ceremonial brewing which takes hours (but time means nothing to these people). We are now at the third glass.

I have promised my razor to Chibani. He seems delighted. He never asks for anything.

Like Villon, I could say :

To Larbi : my good knife bought in the Boulevard de la Madeleine, and which I have never used.

To Chibani : my father's razor, which has lost its edge.

To the sheikh of Tigilit : my binoculars, which he preferred to scrounge.

To three whores of Tigilit . . .

To the earth of Smara . . . &c.

10 *o'clock.*

Lhassen still not here.

But my feet are much better.

Lhassen (and that is why I am not too worried) will certainly increase the number of halts to scrounge a little and guzzle some sugar.

It is to be observed how my liking for them varies. At the end, I will sum up.

* * *

Now, even I also eat goat-flesh that is gamey.

1.30.

Still nobody. I have just had a fit of temper. Lhassen, because his wife is fed here by me, because he also lives on me during the journey, takes four, five days instead of two to make the return journey from the souk.

4 *o'clock.*
Still nobody.

* * *

I find that I am affected by what goes on in precisely the same way as the people of Tigilit. Here they live only on goat flesh (for festivals), barley, maize, milk and dates (compare that with the food of the French peasant, as I fancy it : good milk, cream, brown bread, &c.), and food is their chief concern : they know when a goat is killed in the village, and do all they can to get hold of a piece.

They grow a little maize, very little ; beyond that, they do not work at all. The dates ripen without attention. It is forbidden to gather them before they are ripe. For the rest, the men devote themselves to Moulana [1] and to the women. Make love a great deal. Nearly every night hold some sort of a fête. A few negroes take the goats to the pasturage. The men go when there is a baroud. However, since these become too frequent, it often happens that barley (which they import), goats, money, sugar, and tea are exhausted. Then many of the men leave the oasis and travel north, even as far as French Morocco, leaving the women and children in the lurch.

Tuesday, October 21.
Still at Tigilit.
At seven o'clock, Lhassen had not arrived.

[1] God (literally : ' our Lord ').

8 o'clock.

Chibani just came in. Two men of the neighbourhood report that 300 men, of whom many are mounted
(Aït Moussa or Ali, Aït Lhassen, &c.) have cut the
road between here and the souk. El Mahboul was
not very worried about it, saying that about fifty men
of Tigilit had gone, and have plenty of friends down
there.

Chibani took his rifle and cartridges, and went.

I said ' Labès,' and he answered ' Labès ' (All
right).

* * *

Last night, disgusted by so much delay, I was
thoroughly depressed. So much money thrown to the
winds. Jean interrupted in his work.

Then :

But even if we lose our money on the venture, shall
we also not have changed the pace, the scope of our
lives ? Isn't that the chief thing ? But we must
succeed.

That brought me back to myself immediately.

* * *

All the men of Tigilit, about eighty, have gone
out to meet the caravans.

Chibani did not go to the baroud. All he did
was to take his gun and then make a trip to the
prostitutes' quarter before coming back here.

No meat, no maize to eat : a little barley and
edible gourd, like a pumpkin.

12.30.

Days hard to get through (as are the nights).

Events of the past ; our one outstanding experience ; plans for the future, taken one by one, can hardly move me any more. The crowded present : what is this crowded present worth if I can find nothing to do in the future ?

The uneasiness, the spite, this constant effort to get the better of me and to cheat me.

I take my watch. I calculate again the number of days. I think of the work done. Sometimes a mad spasm of rage which must be overcome ; the days piling up in this wretched hole ; the troublesome flies ; headaches ; lice ; stiffness and sores. And if the camels have been stolen. . . . That sentence I was almost afraid to write.

Every second I strain to catch sight of them, to hear those voices which will bring me back some joy, or plunge me yet deeper into perplexity.

Phrases which come back to me, to make me shudder ; of Aeschylus, I believe : ' Desire nothing too much, lest the jealous gods forbid it.'

And how I desire this thing !

In spite of the gods . . . that is the only reply !

2.30.

Still nothing.

* * *

I have told how Chibani and Muhammed escaped the ambush laid by the ten men of Fask (or Tagant ?).

These bandits, while they were posted on the road,

saw one of the Aït Youssa riding a camel, and drawing
near to them. They killed the Aït Youssa and took
the camel. They have just found the dead body of the
man, gnawed by jackals. As for the camel, the robbers
took it to the souk which has just been held, with an
idea of selling it. But one of their victim's relatives
was there, recognized it, and charged the sellers with
murder. From which arose a fairly complicated tale
of indemnity : the Madani, I believe, compelled the
murderers to pay five hundred francs to the family of
the dead man.

On the other hand, the Aït Chogout sheikh, whom I
distrust increasingly, insists that Chibani ought not
to take part in the expeditions : too old, too easily
tired (Chibani is only forty years old). But Chibani
jeers at his fears.

If the Aït Chogout is too insistent, or if we cannot
come to a better understanding with him, we shall drop
him. Chibani has, in fact, just met one of his relatives
recently returned from Smara. The road is good at
the moment, and what is more, the town is almost de-
populated these days, which will facilitate my work
enormously. I wonder what we should do if we found
several thousand men in and around the town, which
appears to be the case from time to time.

Wednesday, October 22.

Not one of the fifty men who went to the souk has
returned to Tigilit. One is lost in conjecture. They
cannot all have been killed.

The sheikh came back yesterday with his eighty
men, having seen neither the Aït Youssa horsemen

nor the caravans. But they killed two moufflons, of which we received a few pieces.

In this fearful delay, Smara becomes something bitter for me. I am drying up completely, so to speak : my head is full of a single expression of will, which I feel in me, firm, irrevocable : to bring it to an end, to reach my goal ; but, this thought does not bring me any pleasure. I cannot recapture that exaltation which carried me away at other times. I am shrivelled. I have no particle of good nature in me. I can no longer think of my relatives and friends, of the future or of the past. I feel myself cut off, in a solitude that is almost inhuman. One thing only forces itself on me, from which I am not allowed to depart for a moment. I have no more fears : illnesses ; the swollen Dra ; waterless wells ; men of ill will ; chicanery of the sheikhs : nothing of all that. Time no longer matters. I am a little like the gambler who loses, but continues for sheer obstinacy.

1 *o'clock.*

I have looked long enough for this return from the souk, this arrival of the camels ! By one of the loopholes I can see a narrow strip of earth, close up to the mountain, between which and the oued they must pass before entering Tigilit. Last night, about dusk, I was sure I saw them, but it was only goat-herds with their goats, coming in from pasture.

The oasis livens up a little during the evenings. Squatting at the foot of their houses, the men, dressed in blue and white, gather in groups of five or six to gossip. Around the tents (striped light and dark brown), women, and children playing.

One by one, the palm-trees lose their fine fingers of dates. It is the time of the harvest.

* * *

The time when I went to the Aéropostale in the rue de Berry. The conferences at the Geographical Society, at the National. Mornings in rue Cassette at *l'Afrique Française*. The calls on Jean Brunhes, Martineau, Augustin Bernard. The side-excursions : camera, Gaumont. The last purchases.

More recently, the time when I bought peaches for the crossing, at Marseilles, with everything to be begun, to do.

I remember all that with joy, because it is past, because it meant the beginning of action. Now, we are in it. That cheers me a little.

Thursday, October 23. 6 a.m.

I hardly slept during the night, listening for the barking of dogs. Then it grew cold.

A man who arrived during the night, a little ahead of the caravan, told Chibani, who slept near to me (El Mahboul being nobody knows where)—the man spoke from the courtyard—that the Reguibat sheikh had suddenly left the caravan at Aman Aït Youssa (where we ate, opposite Tabaïout), and gone home.

Does he intend to take me prisoner if I move on to Smara ?

We must wait for Lhassen.

8 *o'clock*.

Chibani brings news that the Reguibat sheikh [Embarek] has just this moment reached Tigilit, forerunner of the caravan, which must be here before long. They had camped for the night in the gorges where we stayed to drink, and where the young man of El Bordj, who acted as escort to us, and was later killed, surprised us when we lay flat on our stomachs, with our faces in the water. But the animals were heavily loaded, with barley and sugar, and are spent, it seems. The Reguibat sheikh explained that at Aman Aït Youssa he left the caravan to go as far as the Dra with four of his fellow-tribesmen who were returning home, and that he came back at full speed, travelling all night. He came across two *ifis* (these are most likely hyenas), which he killed.

It seems that things begin to fall into line.

8.30.

Lhassen is not yet here. But several caravanners have reached the town, bringing provisions from the souk. Chibani—(Ali ou Boujma)—borrowed half a loaf of sugar from one of them, and we are now regaling ourselves with tea. Already at the fourth glass (true, they are small !).

12.15.

Lhassen arrived about half an hour ago. I have not seen him yet. They are climbing up to our hovel with the provisions. Fatma Outana pounds pepper in a wooden mortar.

How fine they are, these preparations !

8.30.

We shall not start to-night. The camels, after carrying hundredweights of barley and sugar (most of it for the sheikh), are all in.

Besides, we should rouse too much curiosity among the men of Tigilit if we went on to-night. We expect to leave to-morrow night, about eight o'clock.

My *sebbat* (slippers), which have cost pretty dearly, says El Mahboul (eighty francs, I believe), are soaking in water. . . .

I may leave note-book No. 4 with Bous.[1]

Muhammed has not been able to find a saddle for sale, so that we shall only have the saddle which I used on the previous raid. I think that they will be able to find a second in Tigilit.

* * *

I could not help laughing to myself, as I remembered the somersault the Aït Chogout took near the lake,

---

[1] My brother, in the last pages of this note-book, repeated his advice :

' *Thursday, October* 23.

' MY DEAR JEAN,—I hope to leave to-night for Smara. At last everything seems propitious after so much muddling.

' 1. If I should be captured, let me say again that the sheikh of Tigilit knows everything. I believe he has foreseen the event of the Moors recognizing me for a roumi and keeping me prisoner. He will have me claimed by a second Reguibat sheikh, who will let me escape. For the thirty thousand francs he has guaranteed to get me out of any such scrape.

' Do nothing, on principle (payment of money, &c.), unless you have a letter from me. Except, of course, unless the weeks begin to pile up. But be perfectly sure that I am alive, and the best proof of that will be a letter from me.

' 2. If I should be wounded, and send you word to rejoin me at Tigilit, for example, you can be perfectly sure of Chibani. Failing

situated not far from the Ouargziz, I believe. Just as
the camel was kneeling (and when they are tired the
animals do not do this at all gently), with me behind
the Aït Chogout, I caught him a bump in the back
with my head, which sent him head over heels into
the sand, and nearly into the water. Like a fiend,
he got up as best he could, limping, and stared at me
furiously. As for me, I met his gaze not too badly,
quite seriously, but held my sides for fear I should
burst with laughter : the purler of the swarthy little
fellow was so unexpected and so comic.

3 o'clock.

They were twelve warriors of El Bordj who tried
to ambush Chibani and Muhammed. But they have
always been allies of the Aït Bouhou, and the ambush
was laid because they accuse the sheikh of Tigilit of
sheltering a roumi. They ask for 100,000 francs as
their share of the booty.

him, take Muhammed as a guide and engage half a dozen men to
serve as your escort. I think you would do well to disguise yourself as a woman. In that event it would be advisable for two
women to accompany you, because the escort should be kept in
ignorance.

' But I think that all this is unnecessary. MICHEL.'

' Reckon seven days going to Smara, two days there, seven for
the return to Tigilit, five or six to reach Tiznit.

' 2.30.

' We are not leaving to-night, the camels being worn out ; it
would seem strange to the Arabs. We shall leave to-morrow
evening, about eight o'clock.'

* * *

Note-book No. 4 was delivered to me at the same time as the
letter telling me that my brother had returned.

It seems that the sheikh of Tigilit, enraged by the
affair, has made an official reply to the effect that in
about three weeks (that is to say, when I shall be out
of danger) he will declare war on them, unless (and this
I did not grasp) twelve men come to the marabout, &c.

Fearing that, in the hope of reward, the people of
El Bordj will inform the Madani of my presence, and
of the likelihood of our crossing his territory (which
would certainly make him put a watch on the roads, if
he were informed, and having captured me demand a
ransom of several hundred thousand francs), we intend
to make a detour on the return and avoid his country.

My feet are well on the way to recovery ; but my
stomach and bowels are not in good shape. Still,
there are some advantages. Although perhaps I am
not in such a good state physically, I go armed this
time, the sheikhs are a little better in hand, Chibani
goes with us (and this is capital), the animals belong
to me, I have some provisions of my own, am more
practised with camels, in the handling of the compass,
watch, and camera, my feet will be wrapped. Probably Lhassen will come with us (remembering the
possibility of the baroud, that is not without its value).
We shall have four water-skins and an alibi—the sugar.
We shall not have meat to eat, but that is not so very
important. My important medicines are nearly spent
(antiseptics), and that is really unfortunate.

7 p.m.

About an hour ago Chibani came into the room with
the Aït Chogout sheikh (Ahmed), then El Mahboul,

and, after Chibani had called him, Embarek (the
Reguibat)—his head, which can only be compared to
that of a buck or a vulture, crammed into his blue
turban, his mouth open.

I may seem inconsistent, but it is rather these
impulsive, changeable men who are that. Embarek
came towards me, his hand extended, and shook mine
warmly for perhaps a minute, let go, and took it again
immediately, greeting me in the way of these people :

' All right ? Is it all right ? Really all right ? Then
it is all right ? ' &c.

He wanted to know about my feet, and finally
seemed honestly pleased to see me again, as though
I were his friend, and with every semblance of
sincerity.

Then he sat before the tea-tray with the others :
with one shake of his head he threw his turban behind
him, uncovering his long black hair, thrown back,
leaving his forehead bare.

He made the tea, carrying on a long conversation,
which still goes on, continued by candlelight. (I
must get El Mahboul to tell me what they said.) So
far as I can understand, the sheikhs, still dubious, want
to know why I should be so insistent on Smara, &c.

I spoke very little, only saying :

' I do not wish to stay here any longer. I prefer the
djebel, or Tiznit, or Smara. But to leave here, where
it is as though I were dead, with so little sun, always
crouching . . . lice.'

' . . . It is agreed. I am very tired. Yesterday,
going day and night, I did seventy miles. However,
we will start to-morrow, *in sh'allah* (If God wills).

' . . . You are a real man.'

Then I told him fairy-tales about the sugar and tea, and the warehouses, Jean, &c.

Interrupted by him. While I was writing, he took a sudden fancy to see my feet without their bandages. And it was necessary to show him the sores which were healing. Wanted me to throw everything into the air. Told me that I looked every bit a Moor, that my friends in America would never recognize me.

Then he went over it all again : that Chibani was not to go with us, and he turned sharply to me, to ask me what I thought (Chibani and the Aït Chogout had gone down into the courtyard).

' . . . No, on the contrary, he must go with us. He is an amazing fellow. Like a father to me (*Ouallou, ouallou. Chibani argaz, mezian argaz, kif baba ana*).' [1]

El Mahboul, Embarek, and the two women at the end of the room roared with laughter.

From time to time he seized my hand and shook it. Then—the tale of my bandages, only not so amusing. Then he said good evening (which the Moors and the people of the Dra never do), and left us. A few seconds later he reappeared, asking El Mahboul for a loaf of sugar, which he wanted to present to the prostitute whose tent is placed at the foot of this house, and who is one of his old acquaintances.

They gave him his loaf of sugar.

(Last night, the Aït Chogout sheikh obtained the favours of the lady at the same cost to himself : a piece of moufflon. Only, the giver was the sheikh of Tigilit.)

---

[1] Literally : ' Not at all, not at all. Chibani man, fine man, same as father to me.'

Friday, October 24. 7 *a.m.*

El Mahboul asked if he could buy a goat for seventy francs. It was too dear, he admitted, but for days we have had nothing to eat except barley and pumpkin. I should find it pleasant to eat a little meat myself, and it would put everybody into a good humour. I said he could buy it.

In addition, the sheikh of Tigilit advises us to present two large dishes of couscous, some sugar, tea, and a little meat to twenty men of the oasis. They are beginning to whisper, &c. That El Mahboul can well attend to.

Have I said that one of the reasons the Aït Chogout took the Tigilit road again was to recover the favour of Moulana ?[1] And El Mahboul jibed, ' Do you think that Moulana is more likely to be at Tigilit than at Smara ? '

10 *o'clock.*

What a spell-binder El Mahboul is.

Alone with the Reguibat, who came an hour and a half ago, and made me sit at the end of the room, behind the partition wall, under the pretext that a man had seen me. I refused : lice, &c. He insisted. I had strong suspicions of pederastic tendencies. He, however, ferreted everywhere, finding pieces of meat which El Mahboul had hidden on his arrival, some new slippers, and finally a little cotton bag in which some silver money was kept.

At this moment, Chibani and El Mahboul came back. Both of them flew into a rage, and for an hour there were high words. El Mahboul did not pause

[1] God.

for a moment, gesticulating, spinning it out in an endless stream.

Everything is quiet now, the Reguibat having gone ; brigand that he is, he profited by the quarrel to ask ' three hundred, four hundred thousand francs, a million ! '

' In Casa [1] itself there isn't a million,' said El Mahboul.

Just now it is the Aït Chogout who is questioning El Mahboul, who has not ceased to talk with the same fire and energy, the same volubility. He dazes them, dinning words into their ears, mesmerizing them, putting them to sleep. When the Moors leave here, they are benumbed.

* * *

Bous and Fatma Outana, with the help of Lhassen's wife, sift the barley we are to take with us.

2.30.
Ate a dozen locusts. Red, when they are grilled. One takes off the legs and wings, and eats head, body : taste, as excellent, it seems to me, as I have yet experienced. But to what food are they to be compared ?

* * *

Ludicrous as it may sound, the Aït Chogout is now talking of making the journey from Tigilit to Smara and back in twenty, thirty, or a hundred days, making halts here and there. These people are crazy. All that, I take it, so that they can eat goat-flesh for twenty, thirty, or a hundred days. Or is he looking for some

[1] Casablanca.

subterfuge and evasion so that, while not absolutely
betraying me, he can put me under the obligation of
paying out money, part of which will stick to his
fingers ? How can I tell ?

* * *

I pack. I try on slippers which, such as they are,
are not the least use to me. The leather chafes the
sore places, and in spite of the bandage, I should not
be able to walk. I like those of El Mahboul better,
unless we slit the sides of these.

7 o'clock.

Just as we are on the point of departure, everything
is in the air again. The three sheikhs are talking of
50,000 francs : then, the sheikh of Tigilit, more
reasonable, would be satisfied with 5000, saying that
with 30,000 there is nothing in it for him. El Mahboul
refuses. The sheikh of Tigilit comes down to 2000.
El Mahboul still refuses. Chibani suggests 1000. El
Mahboul is adamant.

It seems, however, that we may be going to get
away.

By the light of two candles, they are putting the
sugar loaves in the sacks, followed by the tea, teapot,
kettle. Barley flour in a skin, so swollen that it has
regained the shape of the animal. El Mahboul has
sewn 1000 francs in his clothes, in case, he says, we
should be separated from Chibani and the others.

I hear that the mehari I used during the first attempt
is at pasturage about twenty miles from Tigilit, and
that the sheikh forgot to send for it until to-day. He

wants us to wait till to-morrow before we start. I refused. El Mahboul refused. We shall have only three animals.

And the Reguibat and the Aït Chogout are not willing to take two saddles, arguing that that would seem suspicious in traders.

V

FROM TIGILIT TO SMARA

Saturday, October 25.

Written on the camel, as it idly grazes the leaves of a bush.

We left Tigilit yesterday about ten o'clock. As I followed Lhassen, who led me by my long robe as we passed along the houses, I said to myself that it was probably the last time that I should walk there ; that I should tread the soil of the oasis (because El Mahboul had given me to understand that we should probably not return by way of Tigilit).

Seeing a man, Lhassen made me go into the dark passage, where I had crouched once before.

This time, nobody in the courtyard.

We flanked the last houses, and followed the river-bed towards the north ; in order to put the too-inquisitive off the scent, the sheikh of Tigilit had decided that we should make a show of taking the road to Goulimin and follow it for about ten miles (twenty miles extra, then).

I took a thousand precautions not to damage my feet among the rocks, trying to find the earth by the light of the stars (no moon). After travelling for perhaps half an hour, in a place where the river-bed is tightly wedged between two high walls of rock . . .

Oued Dra, 11 *o'clock*.

. . . Lhassen came to a halt, and we lay down, among the rocks. I watched the shooting-stars and made my wish. Lhassen was not wide awake, and unless I had been on the look-out would have let the Reguibat sheikh go by, who came on us with velvet tread. Lhassen left us to bring up the camels.

The sheikh and I advanced a little, then stopped. The sheikh handed me dates, then I stole into the shelter of two large rocks. In spite of the rubble, &c., I fell asleep (I had not been able to sleep earlier).

Was I asleep for long? I do not think so. The camels were there, led by El Mahboul—but not loaded. (All these precautions to avoid the animals making a noise and attracting the attention of the people of Tigilit.) I lay down again with El Mahboul, who told me that the negotiations were not ended : the sheikh of Tigilit demanding 2000 francs, the two sheikhs insisting that I do not take Chibani along.

Long wait in the rocks. El Mahboul told me the name of the stars (in Chleuh, naturally). Then the sheikhs wanted to make one of the meharis kneel, to saddle him. He was obstinate, so they decided that I should walk a little. But it was my turn to take things easily. They made me ride bare-back on the beast. But after about four hundred yards, every moment in danger of being pitched among the rocks, I had to get down and continue on foot. It is impossible to describe my rage when I felt the sore on my left foot open up again. I returned to the charge. At last they got the mehari down.

The road, which followed the river-bed between its

walls of rock, soon became easy. But it had been said that I should have to make the crossing of the mountain on foot. My mount, as it was, instead of following the camel ahead, made her way into a blind alley, from which she was unable to extricate herself—rocks on the right and a chasm to the left—except by an acrobatic jump. El Mahboul made me slide into his arms.

I would rather have stayed on the animal, sure that she would have found her way out well enough.

As far as the rise leading to undulating ground, I travelled on foot. One of the animals bought by El Mahboul is with young, and, because she is the one who cries the least, they had put everything on her back. But she was spent, and whenever she came to a rock that needed to be climbed, she screamed in protest.

The three camels were brought to their knees. I mounted mine again, and we continued northwards. The night : well advanced, icy cold. I could almost say Arctic. A penetrating wind. Impatiently I waited for the sun, although I knew that it could not rise for several hours. Travel made most difficult because the saddle, badly fixed, slipped on to the neck of the animal, and I needed to hang on unless I wanted to crack my skull. I found means, by a sudden jerk, to push the saddle back. And then : a mad longing for sleep, which threatened to overpower me at any moment.

Once, after two hours' march in these dales, earth yellowish and hard, some low tufts on the surface, the two sheikhs, Chibani, and El Mahboul lay down, and I was allowed to remain in the saddle. I waited

for a quarter of an hour.   Then, not understanding, I
called them.   El Mahboul told me then that the
Reguibat sheikh did not recognize the trail, and that
they would have to wait for sunrise.   So they had left
me there, shivering, frozen !   I slid into the arms of
El Mahboul and lay down close to him.   In spite of
the cold, which made me shiver, I went to sleep.

El Mahboul awoke me.   The faintest glimmer of
light in the east.   The sun would take an hour and a
half, perhaps, before it was completely risen.   They
tightened the cords of my saddle.   Comfortably
mounted, I could protect myself a little from the cold
by pulling my cloak over my chest.

This time, the way lay full south, then west-south-
west, then west, then south-west, through dales at
first, then the valley—the gorges, I might truthfully
say, of an oued.   The sun struck some parts of the
valleys, but left the others at the mercy of the shadow
and the icy wind.   Crossing these stretches, I looked
eagerly for the line where the shade ceased and the
sun began.   I had nothing with which to drive my
camel, which was a little annoying : he stopped here
and there to browse.   Through how many hands has
he passed ?   How often has he been part of a raider's
booty ?

The sun not only bathed the earth, but warmed me
thoroughly again.   I caught once more the happiness
of pressing on towards my goal, of its near attainment.
The joy of seeing to right and left those avalanches of
rocks, those grandiose gorges, of being the first of my
race to enter ; of thinking of the halting-places, a
stage ended ; of meat to be cooked, &c.

The bed of the river twisted and turned, but kept
its southerly or, better, south-westerly direction.   The
animals were allowed to browse.   Even a fairly long
stay, while the camels ate the leaves of bushes, and
the men some dates.   El Mahboul and the Aït Chogout
brought me more than I could eat.   I put the remainder into the hood of my burnous.   I had something more, besides : a piece of barley bread which I
slipped into my sátchel before we started.   Also,
before we left, although I was not at all thirsty, I
drank as much water as I could (nearly three pints,
perhaps).   And I did well : the water-skins were
empty, and the sheikhs told me that there would be
no water until we reached the Dra, but I was not
thirsty.

We took the road again, along the oued.   At the
end, as I looked, sometimes visible, sometimes hidden,
was a very large range lying east and west, where I
placed the Dra, but which I could not photograph
because of the sun.

At last we came out of that valley and entered
another lying east and west, where the Dra runs :
reeds, running water !   Lying in the grass : tea ;
mint-alcohol ;   goat, almost raw, &c. ;   my feet to
attend to.

We arrived at the course of the Dra some thirty
miles (?) farther west than the other time.

Sunset (watch says 5.30).
[*Half-way down the djebel Mokto.*]

Followed road west-south-west, crossing small range,
and entering country called Zini (Aït Youssa).   Here
and there, hills, sometimes rocky, sometimes covered

with earth, but always bare.   Not riding in the saddle,
but on two hampers, to get used to it.

Saw the Mokto in the distance. After climbing the first
spur, I snatched the chance to take Zini.   Acrobatics.

Saw cistern at the foot of the Mokto.   There, I
changed mounts, no longer on the hampers.   My
saddle, a few moments later, lurched forward on to
the neck, and I scarcely escaped being thrown to earth.
Wrist-work, to put myself on the cruppers.

Ascent of the djebel.   A camel, all in, had to be
unloaded completely.   The Aït Chogout sheikh stayed
behind with the animal, who lay flat on the earth, skin
congested, almost blackened.   We continued the climb.
Examination of an enormous metallic seam, sixteen to
twenty feet high, and miles long.   Took specimens.

Awful wind :   the windy Mokto.   Cold.   Already
icy in the shade, and the sun hardly beginning to set.
Almost blown out of my saddle.   From the top :
marvellous view.   Setting sun.   The line of the
Ouargziz rediscovered.   No photographs.   Descent in
the wind.   Crouched under a rock.   No wind.   Fire.

The Aït Chogout sheikh rejoined us, having left the
camel in the mountain (more than half an hour's
journey).   Is he likely to die ?   We shall know to-
morrow morning.   How are we going to carry our
baggage ?   We shall hide some of the provisions,
which we can find again on the return journey if
to-morrow . . . (night ; night !).

Sunday, October 26.   *Sunrise* (6 *a.m.*).
Same halt.

Yesterday, undoubtedly the strangest evening that
I have spent in my life.   To shield ourselves from the

wind and cold, El Mahboul and I sat in one fault
between two rocks, the sheikhs and Chibani in another.
Lower down these two were joined by a third, deeper
and narrower, where we lit the fire. The smoke and
flames sometimes thrown our way, sometimes towards
the sheikhs ; the glasses of tea which we held over the
flame ; the noise of the wind ; the paste of barley and
arganier oil.

I wrote and reloaded the camera in the gloom.

Night ; doubled up among the rocks ; freezing wind.
Slept. Awoke against El Mahboul.

This morning, the two sheikhs have gone to look for
the camel.

During the night, El Mahboul had a bout of
malaria, I think. Fever — quinine : quinine —
depression.

This morning, Chibani complains of fever. Quinine.

Written on camel-back about 9.30.

Only started at 8.30.

Before that : baking barley bread. Stones in the
fire ; bed of hot bricks ; flour and water ; stones.
Sort of misshapen bread-cake, thick here, flat there.
Tea ; remains of the goat.

But, before that, the sheikhs brought back the
mehari. Found in the same place. Had not moved.
Not even taken a step to find food. Got on to its feet,
and led back by the head. Follows, at the moment,
with an empty saddle and no load. Compare that
with the young she-camel, ears widespread, pendulous
lower lip, working like the devil, always finding the
best path.

We came down into the plain (valley between the

Mokto and the range) and cut south-west to find a pass in the small range.

For eight years, not a drop of water. Thorny tufts, which look as though they had been burned by fire, without a leaf that shows a trace of green. A deeper impression of the desert where life is impossible : stones, black pebbles which look burned, charred. Not always so. Once there were many tents here. To-day, not a man, not a beast (moufflons ; hyenas), not even flies : death. Even the track is avoided by men.

There, where our brother the sun kisses our sister the water, life is born on the earth. Here : sun, the killer.

* * *

The sheikhs, these savages who lock themselves away here.

[12.30 *halt.*]   1 *o'clock.*

March south-west. We crossed the little range, El Mahboul riding behind me, and in that fashion I wrote the preceding pages. We came again to the black stones of the other side, then some sand. Impressive silence. Everybody moved without a word. The noise of our tread was scarcely heard ; the wind only for a moment. When it fell, there was nothing. A few white clouds on high scudded by. Why do you not wait, O clouds ! Why, for eight years, have you never burst into rain ?

Silence broken by an argument which started suddenly among the sheikhs, El Mahboul, and Chibani.

The Reguibat sheikh, for the sake of the camels, suggested that instead of following the direct road south-west we should make a bend and cross the Ouargziz (125 miles extra), so that he could reach his own people, and, if necessary, halt there. The other sheikh wanted, on the other hand, to make a detour to the west, to the place where the Aït Chogout are encamped.

Chibani and El Mahboul put their feet down. The camels are mine, and it would make little difference to me, they said, if they perished, but we are going by the quickest route.

El Mahboul and the Reguibat dropped behind, to argue at length (perhaps El Mahboul promised him money, I do not know, yet). But we kept to the good road.

Going hard enough for me ; perched on the baggage and almost never alone. The Reguibat sheikh and then Chibani climbed up in front.

At 12.30 we came to a halt in a sandy place, where there are a little vegetation (thorny trees, bushes) and . . . flies.

Wonderful march, straight to the south-west, without deviation.

At the halt, the Aït Chogout began his lessons again, teaching me his prayers. ' If you can recite that well,' he said, ' fear neither man nor *ifi* (hyena). You will not be killed.'

Tea, quite good, in spite of the fact that we have carried the water all the way from the Oued Dra, and which tastes like a purgative. . . . (And Chibani called that ' running water ' !)

Same halt.   2 o'clock.

Along the way, Chibani made me a sign, indicating
the Reguibat sheikh with a wink, and at the same time
showing me a cartridge. Not having grasped his
meaning at the moment, I did not make a note of it
previously, thinking that perhaps he meant that the
Reguibat would kill a moufflon if he saw it, or something like that.

The two sheikhs have drawn away a little just at
the moment, and El Mahboul has explained. Nothing
was agreed while they argued in the rear. The
Reguibat still insisted on our taking the route to the
east of this one.

' Why ? ' asked El Mahboul.

' There is water, we shall be able to get camels, &c.'

' But that means that we shall have to do an extra
hundred and twenty-five miles. Let us get to Smara
first, and from there we can go your way, and the
roumi (I don't know how they speak of me among
themselves) will tell you where to find water if you
dig.'

The Reguibat believes I have this ability.

But the Reguibat was obdurate.

We are to stay here until about four o'clock, after
which we shall be on the march throughout the night.
To-morrow we hope to find water. But the Reguibat ;
is he going to be willing to follow us ? El Mahboul
tells me definitely that the territory through which
the Reguibat wants to take us is that of the caid Ali
of the Aït Youssa. What did the sheikh tell his
Reguibat friends as he came back with them from the

souk ? That thought occurred to Chibani and El
Mahboul when the sheikh insisted. The Aït Chogout
himself is chary (Ali, caid of the Aït Youssa, could
demand a ransom of two hundred, three hundred
thousand francs), and says that if the Reguibat is not
amenable to reason, Chibani ought to put a bullet
in his head.

Just now, as we were alone for a moment, El Mahboul
explained all that to me. I can see for myself the
threatening attitude, the sidelong glances of the
Reguibat, as he makes the tea. He is plotting something in his ugly head.

Should he leave us, we will make about thirty miles
with the camels and, abandoning them (to throw the
others off the trail), bear to the west, picking up the
trail to Smara later. If either here or at Smara the
Reguibat is obviously treacherous, El Mahboul informed me, Chibani is ready to put a bullet through
his brain, and wants to know what I think about it.

I told him that I was quite with him, and I went so
far as to say that he needs only to give me the signal
the moment we are in danger, and I will make the
execution myself, from behind or in front, without the
least compunction.

This, to show how much I am in agreement.
Besides, it would be much easier for me than for
Chibani, on whom the Reguibat keeps a watchful eye.

Monday, October 27. 9.45 halt.

Yesterday, halted until four o'clock (my watch is
perhaps an hour slow, because the sun, if I am correct,
sets between five and six).

At first, alone on the camel. Then behind Chibani.

We had to keep going through the night, and I cannot describe the impression made on me by the setting sun ahead, which will rise again behind me while I travel steadily across the same plain, so vast, bounded on right and left by parallel ranges.

Night almost impenetrable. The moon in its first quarter. As soon as darkness fell, the sheikhs and Chibani slipped cartridges into the breech of their guns.

The earth was composed of sand, hard or crisp, gullied in places, which the camels refused to cross. We did not drive them through it, and it was necessary for them to make long detours. Chibani, about seven o'clock, dismounted and continued on foot. But almost immediately he had a bout of fever (as was the case during the day : I do not remember that I noted it). He lay for a moment flat on the ground. I found some quinine and handed it to El Mahboul, unable to open the tube.

While he was busy with it, and walking with the Aït Chogout and Chibani around the she-camel, a hiss (like the escape of compressed gas) burst out just under me, between the feet of the camel. The men scattered, dancing about and shouting. (I shall remember the shrill cries of Chibani.) I drove my mount away from the snake. The men were safe and sound, but the camel? It was night, we could not examine it immediately. If she had been bitten, we should only have the young camel left, over-tired because over-burdened, and neither food nor water. The other mehari followed, with no load except the saddle ; that is to say : nothing ; but sick, flanks covered with sweat.

At eight o'clock we came to a halt on Chibani's account. They lay out the sack, striped light and dark brown, in which are the dates and other provisions, and stretched him on it. Unfortunately the sand was hard. We found a spot where the sand was a little softer, and there I lay with El Mahboul. . . . Cold night.

Awoke at a quarter to five, and on our way. Immediately we rose, in five minutes, the camels were loaded. I had hardly time to put on my slippers. . . .

Dawn cold. Feet and knees bare ; frozen. Alone on the big she-camel. Sand-dunes where the camels buried themselves . . . the sand broke away under them, and they made astonishing slides. The Aït Chogout clambered up in front of me without stopping the camel, and I had to stay for four hours like that, without moving, calves and thighs horribly stretched. I was in a towering rage. The Aït Chogout shifted, changed his position, planted his gun in my ribs. I took good care to give him a jolt or two with my knees and my head ; but, being badly placed as I was, they were feeble and he did not seem to feel them.

Still travelling south-west, I only saw, on either hand, the ranges parallel to the Mokto and the Ouargziz, these latter disappearing behind. Glimpse of gazelles, five or six, which scampered off as we passed.

The whole of this stage was dominated by the effort I had to make. About half-past eight, on our left, we saw a palm-tree and a few ruined houses at the foot of the mountain. I asked what they were. El Msiid, Chibani told me ; a Reguibat oasis destroyed by the

Aït Youssa.   Once numbered several hundred palm-
trees. They were cut down, only one remains. We
passed before the ruins (which I could not photograph
because of the sun facing me), and a few hundred
yards later we inclined to the left, through a very
verdant pass going deep into the range. There we
found water. But it was a well-travelled area : we
discovered traces of the *djich* which was making the
baroud the other day (first attempt).

Numerous goat tracks. A little farther on, camel
tracks. We watered the camels, filled the water-
skins, and moved on. I got down for a few moments
and made a few paces, with great difficulty. I was
so wrenched.

We came out of the pass and regained our road
parallel to the range. Alone on the camel ; El
Mahboul and Chibani blackguarding the Aït Chogout
for having made me ride behind.

At a quarter to ten we came to this halt under
bushes which give no shelter from the sun. Ate a
few dates as I rode the camel. Here : tea and barley
with arganier oil. We are moving on again.

12.45 *halt.*

Started again at half-past eleven. Alone on the
young she-camel. Another argument as to the route
we shall take. Sun, which gave me a slightly quicker
pulse. Still the same desert : sand, pebbles, a few
bushes. Frequent signs of hyenas : glimpse of a hare.
At the end of the plain, two or three hills which stood
alone, with wide passages between them. Did they
mark the end of the enormous, level valley ?

(Photograph, but sun rather badly placed.)

At a quarter to one, while I thought we were on the march until nightfall, a halt ; one of those resting-places which come near to being paradise : shade ; hardly any flies ; a gentle breeze ; a bed of wonderfully soft sand, which gently moulds itself to the shape of the body. After the stiffness and the sun, it is something the like of which does not exist elsewhere, which is only experienced, only won, here ; like water, meat, or even tea.

5.30 p.m. halt.

Rose after the siesta at about four o'clock. Walked a little, in search of the camels. I took the opportunity to collect a few sprigs from three trees.

I rode the sick mehari, which seems to be improving. Saddle, real rest. We travelled on, south-west. The range on our left, quite near ; that on the right, on the contrary, almost out of sight on the edge of the vast plain. The view blocked to the south-west by some small hillocks.

We have stopped to eat a little. I put my photographs in order, &c., and am going to open a tin of peaches, even though I do not really need them. Big fire of brushwood.

Tuesday, October 28. 9.45 *halt.*

At yesterday's halt, where I wrote the foregoing, I ate a tin of peaches, then some barley bread made by the sheikhs (soaked in arganier oil), and, before and after, three glasses of tea.

We got under way in the night, towards the south-west. Moon somewhat larger. I rode the young she-camel, astride sometimes, and could think at my ease. I find much pleasure in these reveries.

The pace of the camel, carrying me gently ahead, towards the goal ; the slight swaying of the body, not painful, all work done ; compass checking direction ; eyes to right and left and ahead, to define the bearings ; the sandy earth making it possible to travel without jolts ; the scenery always the same (the range for landmark to the left, the plain on the right), which gave me leisure ; the night, which made photography out of the question.

Completely at my ease, I could recall our walk with Jean to the island in the Bois de Boulogne, when we were still only people who were going to undertake an expedition to Smara.

I conjured up, with some emotion, my return to Tiznit. All that I should have to say, not only of the present or of the past, but how I regard the future. I pictured the very minute when we should see each other again. . . . Those marvellous moments, for which I always pay by a fit of depression, so intensely am I moved.

Then, weariness came strongly over me, and there remained only the monotonous march.

To the left, the range began to end. On my right I tried in vain to see how far the plain stretched, a plain which seemed immense in the light of the moon.

The moon lit up a few isolated hills ahead of us, lying just across our line of march. To the right of these hills : the plain.

At half-past nine we made a halt. Fine sand ; still warm.

The first moments of settling to sleep were very pleasant. Unhappily, I awoke several times during the night, to discover that my cloak was wringing wet. I was cold myself; but the sand that had not been covered by my body was frosted. I stayed awake from about four or five o'clock, to the time we started.

The good saddle put me right again. I was frozen.

We went into the hills that I had seen during the night by moonlight. Pass, which took us towards the south, then towards the east, opening on to a wide plain, to the right and left of which were disconnected hills, lying, I think, east-north-east by west-south-west.

The sun rose while we were in the pass, but the cloudy skies prevented my taking photographs, which put me in a bad humour, because all this is hard to describe. I am obliged to simplify it.

Travelled quickly south-west. The Reguibat alone was on foot. Often the animals went at the trot. Mine stumbled, and fell cruelly on its side, luckily throwing me clear, on to the stones. Otherwise my leg might have been wedged under the animal. The Reguibat lifted me up. I was badly bruised. I checked up my bag : nothing broken. Into the saddle again.

Large vales. We found a little vegetation and loose sand at the bottom of one, but were disagreeably surprised to see a considerable number of tracks—of camels, goats, and men who had spent the night there (travelling in the opposite direction to us). Two or three thousand men, El Mahboul told me. The whole of a tribe. The sheikhs were uneasy, fluttering about on the high ground. We continued our march as far as a large water-hole, where we came to a halt.

But, if we are to continue our march, the sheikhs have asked me if I will agree to be put in a hamper, like sugar. I agreed, for a short while.

1 p.m. halt.

I was put into a wicker hamper towards midday. Almost immediately I realized that it was not going to be amusing—when they tightened and trimmed the ropes, and, the beast having risen, somebody rammed his shoulder against the hamper where I was, to re-mount, so that the top was sealed at the same time.

A thick woollen burnous thrown over my head protected me from the strong sun, but stifled me at the same time.

There, in the hamper, I was folded back on to myself like a foetus. That shell, that absolute powerlessness to make the slightest movement, hand or foot; strangling, almost agonizing when, finding it necessary to move my bruised foot, I found it impossible to do so.

I was forced to stay exactly as they had stowed me.

At first I bore it tolerably well, then I felt every muscle of the beast go backwards and forwards as it moved. Annoying, and finally painful. Then my shoulder was trapped. That was the hardest. How-ever, I did not dream of getting out of the basket. We had hardly gone a mile before we fell in with a com-pany of about a hundred men getting ready to eat, near to their grazing beasts. I heard voices, a few words exchanged. El Mahboul translated them for me a little later.

THE YELLOW DESERT OF THE GA'A
OCTOBER 30, MORNING

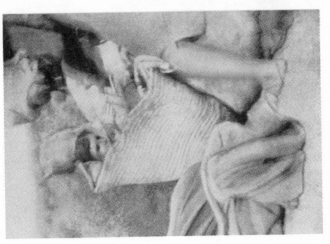

MICHEL VIEUCHANGE TAKING HIS PLACE
IN A PANNIER
OCTOBER 28

' *Salaam aleykoum* ' (Peace be unto you).

' *Salaam.* '

' Have you any sugar ?   We'll buy it.'

' We have no sugar ' (said the Aït Chogout).

' And who is he ? ' (indicating El Mahboul).

' A holy man who has friends in this district.'

And on we went.

About a mile farther on, they made the camel kneel, and Chibani settled me more comfortably. I was almost at ease, I swear, coming to this point near to water.

(The presence of abundant water in this neighbour-hood attracts men—and flies.)

Only my feet, wedged at the bottom of the wicker-work, made me suffer (increased possibly by my futile efforts to find a more comfortable position for them) ; then, when the animal knelt, my back was banged forcibly on to the stones.

When the men were at a safe distance, they uncovered my head, and I was able to check our direction, but that was all.

Rested at one o'clock, among bushes, near to a large lake.

5.45 *p.m. halt.*

En route at a quarter to four. Plain strewn with pebbles. In places, greenery and water. The sheikhs at first wished to travel only at night, then to put me into a hamper, and suddenly decided to go on, with me on the young camel.

But the Aït Chogout had stuffed himself with dates,

barley, and arganier oil, and took a bath on the top
of that. Result : a bout of fever. For which reason,
instead of travelling on, we camped at a quarter to six.
These fellows are really stupid.

Wednesday, October 29. Same halt.
6.45 *a.m.*

Night here. Slept only a few hours after having
eaten a sort of barley stew, abundantly peppered, of
Chibani's making. So annoyed that we could not go
on, by this new delay, that I could not go to sleep
again. The night was cool and damp, not too cold.
In addition, I surprised a suspicious animal once or
twice (scorpion ?) which was crawling on the sack
under my head, and which scurried off when I moved.

In the dead of night, several times I heard Chibani
asking the Aït Chogout if we could start again, and the
other refuse. About three o'clock, however, the
Reguibat (Embarek) got up and made tea. Our
gathering round the fire at night. Embarek rose and
went to find the camels. Came back almost immediately saying that we could not start, the she-camel
having a wound in her foot, limping horribly, and
that we should have to wait till morning for him to
make an examination. We lay down again and I
slept a little.

The day broke, but there was no sun. Fire, and
barley stew again. Then, armed with an awl which
he uses to make his sandals, and a knife, the Reguibat
went to the she-camel lying on a bed of stones. One
by one he took these away, and then tied the fore-
feet and passed a leather strap under the stomach of
the camel and over her buttocks, turning the beast

over. The Aït Chogout sat on her head. The
Reguibat with his awl probed the foot. Found
nothing. The camel floundered about, struggling.
Rid of her bonds, she stood on her feet, limped, and
then seemed to suffer no more, and walked as before.

3 p.m. halt.

In the saddle since seven o'clock, or rather on the
sack in which the sugar and dates are carried, without
respite.

Country of hillocks, with water in the hollows ;
vegetation. That suggested that there were likely to
be travellers. The Reguibat sheikh walked ahead,
and I admired his strong legs, with muscles well
covered—thin ankle, notwithstanding. He went at
a rattling pace, gun slung across his shoulder, held
by the barrel ; erect, his voluminous blue-and-white
robes waving, sandals made of camel-skin on his feet.
This blackguard of a man, of medium height, is a
bit of a savage, an animal made for doing a hundred
miles in twenty-four hours. Between stages, he
swallows pounds of barley (a goat a day, he says, if
he got the chance). Never stops : makes the fires ;
loads the beasts. Almost always on foot. Lisps.

At that moment he was walking in the van, very
quickly, dashing to the tops of the hillocks, scanning
the horizon, shielding his eyes with one hand, showing
us the way with his arm and then scurrying down.

We saw water frequently, but the sheikhs went on
without stopping. They said there was plenty of
water on our trail.

Just the same, the hillocks, which we crossed interminably, became pebbly, the passes separating them

had a few trees but no water. Twice we dropped
down to the verdure, but found no water-hole.

The Reguibat still wanted to leave the road to the
south-west and take a westerly direction (we are in the
Reguibat country). Chibani and the Aït Chogout
protested.

He, without worrying about us, continued to climb
a hill in the direction he wanted us to take. At the
top, he made signs to us ; but Chibani continued
south-west, and the Reguibat was lost to sight.

Where had he gone ? He had no barley ; but
what did that matter to such an old fox ? Chibani
with wide gestures cursed him, berating him strongly,
saying to me : ' Let him go ! Let him go ! '

. . . Is he seeking contact with the Moors of his
tribe, to tell them that a roumi is travelling the
country ? Who knows ? I called El Mahboul and
told him that we must make a forced march to-night
and to-morrow : day and night. In that way we
could reach Smara the day after to-morrow, in the
morning. Once my work is done there, it seems to
me that an enormous weight will have been taken off
my shoulders. Then I could concentrate on taking
care of myself. I will go there, whatever happens.
Then I don't care whether we go south, or to Tindouf,
or even Cap Juby. At present, each detour, each
falling back, each delay is insupportable. That
is why I am glad that the miles pile up, that the
distance separating me from my goal lessens, in spite
of the fatigue among those pebbly hills : sometimes
sliding on to the neck of my mount, sometimes hanging
on so that I did not take a toss backwards ; in spite
of the painful chafings, particularly sensitive when the

animal went at the trot almost to the bottom of every
descent : and this for eight hours, without pausing
for a second.

I do not want them to stop. I have no wish to sleep.
The nearer I get, the more am I possessed by fears.
To-night . . . will they steal the camels ? I can only
hear two. . . . Then, the foot of the she-camel . . .
now the Reguibat. I press our march towards the
goal as much as I can.

Every day now, the sun only appears very late,
towards nine or ten o'clock (water in condensation ?),
and I storm because I cannot take a photograph.

When I have a good view of the road to be covered,
or of the country, the sun in a good position, and myself
not too much jolted ; or when, at the top of a rise I
snatch a moment before the descent, on the crest (the
line, O Gide !) ; or, turning round, I comprehend the
country behind me, and press the release, I find a lively
pleasure.

Two hundred miles deep in a country not yet
explored, I say to myself ; as big as the third of France ;
and these scenes, which nobody has seen, are caught
and held by the camera.

Reloaded the camera on the march for the first time.

The sheikh having left us, we followed a fairly
narrow valley where the air was heavy with incense.
I asked what it was that spread this marvellous
perfume. They showed me a plant ; absinth, I
believe. The camels would only move when they felt
the whip. At the least tuft they dropped their long
necks to nibble a few spikes.

I was alone in the saddle. The sick mehari moved to right and left, hindering my progress. But the sight of the saddle at my back gave me the idea of taking it to Paris : mounted on feet, it would make a good seat.

Towards three o'clock, quite unexpectedly (we ought not to have found water for another ten miles), we saw a pool of water in a hollow. Immediately the animals were knelt and unloaded. A meal was prepared. I dismounted, and moved painfully ; I was so stiff, my back so sore. . . . I imagine what I am writing reads like it.

Same halt. 4 o'clock.

The Reguibat has returned. The Aït Chogout saw him afar off. Behind the bush where I am, I heard his steps. On arrival here he said, ' *Salaam aleykoum.*' ' *Salaam,*' we replied. He sat. Several minutes of silence, then a lively argument burst out. I like that better.

Terrible headache. Feverish, although I am full of quinine.

Bread has just been baked. Chibani, taking it out from under the stones, showed it to me in triumph, and asked me to take a photograph. I agreed instantly, of course. He flourished it proudly, as you [1] will see. Then, hardly a moment later, this bread, which had been immortalized by the lens, was broken into pieces, soaked in arganier oil, and disappeared into our stomachs. That was our meal.

[1] See note, p. 135.

Thursday, October 30.   12.30 *p.m. halt.*

Left at five o'clock, still travelling among the hillocks. The sun as it set illumined their crests, but had left the passes which we followed in the shade. They grew larger. Climb ; and I found myself looking at an enormous panorama under the setting sun. Not enough light [for photography]. And, almost immediately, a sheer descent which was not to be taken lightly. A broad valley from east to west (valley of the Oued Chebi, El Mahboul said), at the bottom of which the sun was setting, making it possible to perceive a vast plain, the Ga'a desert, as I know now.

The descent was accomplished quickly ; by me, little by little, held by what I saw : below, on every side the sombre crests of mountains silhouetted against the clear sky, like the teeth of a saw. In the far distance there was a rosy glow from which beams, scarcely more brilliant than the sky, radiated in every direction.

Standing alone, a dark outline in the glow, and above the low vegetation of the valley which already mingled with the darkness, was an immense palm-tree : isolated.

The line of mountains, like a flight of stairs which moved towards the sunset, the palm-tree, the rosy glow ; beyond which lay that unknown upon which I am to enter ; fascinated me, charmed me immensely, the while my camel continued its way across the bushes from which the gloom surged in a solid mass, like the sides of mountains.

I lived in that blissful state as long as it endured ;

but the glow faded, the palm-tree passed, and the moon, already high, brought other shadows, put another face on the earth.

Slow crossing of the valley, which still continued, as though the mountains kept pace with us. A strong wind in our faces presaged the end of the valley, and almost at once the plain was before us ; infinite under the moon.

From west, we resumed our way south, slightly south-west ; but, almost at the same time, and scarcely a hundred yards away, among the bushes on the edge of the plain we saw, some of us, one fire ; some, two. Men were there. They had no tents, and therefore they were not peaceful caravanners but warriors, with neither faith nor law, hunting for plunder, or on the track of a caravan (there were many fresh traces of camels on the ground ; a caravan travelling south). In that case, we were at the mercy of our camels. The least cry, and the Moors would be after us.

While the Reguibat went ahead among the bushes, rifle at the ready, to see if he could find out anything about the men in the shade, we continued our march quietly, following the foot of the mountains. Not a movement to guide the camels ; they went alone : not a move in the saddle ; immobility. Mine began to kneel, but changed its mind.

Slowly we increased the distance between us and the fires. At about eight hundred yards, very gently, we pulled up the camels, to await the return of the Reguibat.

Having no switch, I was unable to control my mount, which wandered here and there from bush to bush, taking me along with her, much farther than I

liked. We waited for perhaps a quarter of an hour,
which seemed ages to me, always afraid of a cry from
my camel. At last the sheikh caught us up. He had
gone as near as he could, had seen no tent. Therefore
it must be a djich [1] (undoubtedly Aït Lhassen). However, the sheikh was of the opinion that they were not
after the caravan whose tracks we saw—these, to his
mind, were at least a day and a half old, perhaps two
days ; but, if they discovered the new traces left by
us, riding superb animals, they would be on us in a few
hours.

We took up our march again : south, slightly west.
The mountains disappeared. On every side was the
plain, covered with bushes. We drew near a solitary
rock, standing sheer in the plain. At its base, a lake
where we refilled the water-skins. I left the back of
the young she-camel and mounted the mehari, behind
the Aït Chogout, who had complained that he could
no longer travel on foot.

On our way again. The bushes thinned ; the earth
at first of hard sand and later of dry, cracked clay. . . .
Under the light of the moon, one would almost have
said it was a pavement laid by the hands of men. We
were beginning the desert of the Ga'a.

Every hundred yards, the Reguibat sheikh or Chibani
stopped, crouched near the surface of the earth, and
looked to the rear, to see if we were being followed.

Everything round us was absolutely flat, without
the slightest irregularity, without even a solitary bush.
Rump and back battered, legs abominably stretched
apart, I could not bear my position on the cruppers
for more than an hour, riding astride. At the risk

[1] Party of armed bandits.

of a fall, by standing perfectly upright, I succeeded in putting both legs on the same side of the animal. Sitting, I slid towards the tail, and had to hang on to the ropes that secured the baggage.

I was perishing from weariness, and from want of sleep.

At midnight we took a little rest, the camels lying at our sides. I spread a sack on the earth and stretched out, welcoming as an unheard-of blessing the fact that I might sleep.

El Mahboul near to me, we talked for some minutes.

' . . . If we are on the point of being overtaken,' I said, ' we two will leave the camels with my baggage, and try to hide, and Chibani will come back to look for us. . . .'

' . . . If we are overtaken,' replied El Mahboul, ' those two sheikhs, the swine, will sneak off like moufflons and leave us to it. . . .'

' . . . And Chibani ? '

' . . . *Man 'arf* ' (I do not know).

Almost immediately I was asleep, and slept, feeling neither cold nor lice until El Mahboul roused me. It was a quarter-past three.

At half-past three we started again, with myself, as usual, riding behind the Aït Chogout. Several times I checked up our direction. South, slightly west, and sometimes straight south-west. Monotonous going, when all that mattered was to try to shift position in the saddle. The earth, sometimes finely fissured like a mosaic, sometimes like a pavement of our streets

but hard, where the feet of the camels left no traces :
favourable to our flight.

First light in the east. I watched for the arrival
of the sun, to take a photograph, not knowing when we
should arrive at the end of the desert. Sitting on the
side of the camel, I had my back to the east. Several
times I turned round, but suddenly I saw that low
wave of light sliding over the surface of the earth, very
quickly, and covering it entirely, like a flood. Our
shadows seemed enormous. A little later, when the
sun was a shade stronger, I took a photograph, and
El Mahboul one of me. That was lucky, because, a
little later, clouds obscured the sky.

Then the sun reappeared a little more strongly (two
photographs), and finally with great force.

Before me, pieces of water spread out, like a great
sea with islands of dry land ; mirage.

On the earth, tracks of camels that had passed that
way on days when there was rain.

At last we saw the end of the huge desert : some
trees in the distance. Chibani and the Reguibat
hurried ahead to prepare the halt. The animals were
at the end of their powers. The sick camel (carrying
no load) may possibly have to be abandoned in the
Seguiet el Hamra, where we shall be in some hours.
If he is not stolen, perhaps we shall find him again.
The camel who is with young is exhausted, as is the
small camel. But I believe we have escaped from the
djich.

Here at half-past twelve. As soon as the barley
had been eaten, everybody lay down and went to
sleep. I alone stayed awake to write this and to

reload the camera. We are now on the point of
moving on again. I have not time, even, to look at
my feet or my back. But I had to spend some time
taking a thorn from the foot of the Aït Chogout.

3.15 *p.m. halt.*

We started again at two o'clock.

The desert plain stretched on, with a few irregularities of surface. Black soil, stony. Scorching sun,
which beat like a flail on my back, laid me flat on my
mount. However, everybody was happy, since we
seemed to have got away unobserved. Chibani, to
give vent to his joy, danced a jig, which winded him
for a quarter of an hour.

Stretching into the distance : sand and bushes. In
one of these patches of earth we came to a halt at a
quarter-past three. Stage travelled on the young
she-camel.

Here, I have refilled my satchel with quinine and
films ready for the Seguiet and Smara. But the
Seguiet will probably be reached during the night.
On the return I shall make some effort to reach it in
daylight. Collected a few specimens of the flora.

I like these days, these halts when every moment
is precious, where everything that I do counts.

6 *p.m.*

Sunset. Written on the camel. Every time I
try to find something in the satchel it is as though
I assisted at a confinement.

Flaky stones of a dark green colour cover the earth. Debris. Gazelles in sight.

The title for this must be, 'How wonderfully we escaped.'

Chibani, El Mahboul tells me, trembled like a leaf yesterday. And I had believed him an old dare-devil.

Friday, October 31. 8 *o'clock halt.*

[Last night,] left at half-past five. Setting sun. Alone on the young she-camel. Pleasant going. Moon among the clouds. All the stars dimmed. On the horizon : a clearer sky.

Still the desert, except that in place of a yellow desert it had become the black desert. Not that the earth had changed its nature—at least, I do not think it had—only the clay was covered with the remains of flaky stones, greenish or black, of which the scattered hillocks on the black plain are made. In great white patches, the clay was bare, without any stones, and in the night that gave an undulating appearance to the earth, which in reality it does not possess. You got ready for a descent and found the road still level.

The moon, occasionally hidden, and high in the sky, no longer served the sheikhs as a guide ; and not a star, not a natural landmark (valleys, &c.). A few chance hillocks rising here and there.

Compass in hand, or laid before me on the camel, I saw that the Reguibat, marching ahead, went wrong, having lost his direction. For one moment we moved to the north. I warned El Mahboul and the Aït Chogout, both riding the female mehari.

' This is the way to Tigilit ! Look, the sea is
there. That is the line of the sun's travel. Smara
is there ; the Seguiet there ; this is the proper
direction. . . .'

The Aït Chogout sheikh told the Reguibat as he
squatted on the ground, scanning the horizon here and
there. Discussion, which lasted several minutes. My
camel passed them, and I heard the Aït Chogout,
astounded that I should know where I was, and that I
could point out the way to Smara, laughing in the
night, and repeating, with wonder and a little mockery,
to the Reguibat :

' *Oualou, oualou ! Menna Tigilit !* ' [1]

The Reguibat sheikh, taking advantage of my
advice, took a direction full south, or very, very slightly
to the west. I kept my compass open all the time.
He disappeared into the night. Then, at a moment
when I was unexpectant, suddenly reappeared at the
feet of my camel. Sitting there on the ground, I had
taken him for some discoloration of the earth.

About ten o'clock, the hillocks grew closer together ;
we followed the passes. Then, after argument between
the sheikhs and Chibani, we stopped. The Seguia
being close at hand, Chibani refused to approach it
during the night, fearful of falling across an encampment. They unloaded the beasts and we lay down
. . . hard earth.

Roused at six a.m. and started, the sheikhs believing
the Seguiet very near ; but we marched for a long time
across the black hillocks—until about eight o'clock.
Saw gazelles, and, at eight o'clock . . .

[1] ' No, no !   That is the way to Tigilit ! '

11.30 *a.m. halt.*

. . . in the opening between two hills, appeared a
vast valley with yellow earth covered with bushes and
thorny trees ; the Seguiet, El Mahboul told me.

Soon, our camels trod this yellow, clayey earth,
deeply fissured, and with pools of water, bushes, and
grass. They immediately began to browse, for two
days denied good grazing and water. I dismounted
and, not knowing whether we were to cross the
Seguia at once, I went straight to one of the hillocks
which border it and took two photographs, taking
advantage of the brief appearances of the sun between
the clouds.

Coming down, the sheikhs greeted me with a stream
of words and gesticulations. El Mahboul said that if
I kept on running here and there I stood the risk of
signalling our presence, and that we might all be
killed : the sheikhs having no friends in this territory,
where the Reguibat, Izargiin, and Aït Youssa are
interlocked like the fingers of praying hands. It was
impressed on me that we were in the Seguia itself, and
that I must not go far away.

We drank three glasses of tea, then started again at
ten o'clock, but this time the sheikhs insisted on putting
me in the pannier. There were three thousand tents
of the Reguibat in the neighbourhood. And, in addition, a great number of fresh tracks on the earth, in all
directions. I had to make up my mind. So again
behold me doubled up, knees up to my chin, head
awkwardly placed and hanging backwards.

And they stayed where they were !

The sheikhs, from the top of one of the hills, watched

a group of about thirty horsemen, whom they had discovered encamped at about five hundred yards' distance. I was left wedged against the flank of the animal, which moved in fits and starts across the gullies of the Seguia, stopping here and there to graze. El Mahboul might have been anywhere ; Chibani also. I could not see the other two camels. Glued to the beast, as though I were part of her, we were alone among the hillocks and bushes. According to where she grazed, my head was in sun or shade—a frightful sun which I could not escape : arms tightly wedged in the hamper.

I called El Mahboul. Nobody replied.

(He was peacefully in the shade with Chibani, two hundred yards away.)

It seemed to me that I had my eyes turned to the sky, that I was a creature who walked backwards, by jerks. In that fashion, I saw the yellow embankments of the Seguia file past, at some yards—or inches—and the low trees whose branches banged my head. I kept calling, not daring to raise my voice too much.

Finally, El Mahboul ! I called him all the names I could think of : ' You are an ass, &c.'

The poor fellow was not to blame : it seemed quite natural to him. Immediately he wanted to stop the march, to let me rest. I had a lot of trouble in calming him, still fearing some sudden about-turn by the sheikhs, whose strange movements Chibani was signalling to El Mahboul.

While waiting for them, they made my camel lie down. My loins bore directly on the hard earth, and that was no joke.

Finally, they returned and we started again. The

men they saw seemed peaceful : they had goats and tents.

We are going to build a fire and take some food here. After a few more minutes' travel, we stopped and I was freed from my shell. It is eleven-thirty.

Sitting in the shade, I wrote, while my men argued among themselves. I was at a loss to know how to quieten the uneasiness. The Reguibat looked the most dangerous, the angriest. I took the wooden compass and went to him :

' Do you want to know why I told you last night that Smara lies this way ? Look at this. Always in that place, the needle pointing here, you will find the sea. I will give it to you, and then, never, never will you be in doubt.'

El Mahboul explained to him ; but he pushed the compass aside and lay down, his head hidden under his arms.

' . . . What is the matter with him ? '

Furiously he spoke to El Mahboul :

' . . . I know where Smara is. The roumi says that he knows. He doesn't know. It is false ; he lies.'

I had wounded his pride. I beat a retreat to my satchel. Chibani was ashamed of the sheikh, who then seemed to understand what had happened and smiled at me, offering me some dates. I have just told him again that I think he is wonderful, that I do not know where Smara is, but only the position of the sea.

At present, I am sitting on the hard clay, my feet wrapped in my cloak, to protect myself from flies.

Piping of birds.   The sheikhs are washing the saucepan and making a fire.

So at last I have reached the Seguiet, that long line I saw on the maps : I am there, with Smara close by : close to the goal.

Some explanation is needed : The Seguiet has the appearance of a vast plain, about six miles wide, yellowish earth, red in places, covered with bushes.

6 p.m. halt.   9 o'clock.

Written by moonlight.   Cannot sleep.   Two or three hours' sleep are enough for me now.   This new delay just when we are reaching the oasis worries me. A little while ago, utterly destitute of happiness, utterly void, I opened a box of cherries.

Moved on at a quarter to three.   Sun.   I was put into the hamper.   I stayed there for an hour, until we reached the middle of the Seguia, which we were crossing.   A frightful hour : my arms bruised ; my sides ; my knees cramped one against the other ; my feet asleep ; retching.   I did not want them to stop. It was Chibani who, seeing my face bathed in perspiration, shouted, ' But he is dying in there ! ' (*L'mout mena !*), and brought the camel down and drew me out with the help of the Aït Chogout.   It was a minute before I could walk.

Finished the crossing of the Seguia on the young she-camel.   Nearly all the vegetation and water are collected on the bank we reached first.   On the side where we are at present, some low bushes are scattered thinly over the arid soil, no grass.   The land rises very slightly on the far side.

We came again to dales covered with broken black stone. The Reguibat sheikh, who was ahead, came back to us. He had seen a large number of tents, camels, goats, and men. . . . Izargiin.

Into the hamper again. The Aït Chogout wanted to find out what was going on. He looked for a small group of men, but failed to find them, and returned. The sheikhs decided not to start again except in daylight. Crossed the Oued el Maïriz. They made a halt at about six o'clock, and I came out of the hamper. Soft sand. Weary ; blown ; feverish.

Saturday, November 1. *All Saints' Day.*
[Same halt] 7.30. *Oued el Mairiz.*

Spent the night here. The nights still grow icy towards the end. At daybreak : tea and barley cakes soaked in arganier oil. The sheikhs went off to examine the neighbourhood. One of them (the Reguibat) says that the country is full of men. When are we likely to get away from here ?

8 o'clock.

The Reguibat sheikh and Chibani, later joined by El Mahboul, from the stones of a tomb, have built a sort of little fortress on one of the hills bordering the oued, a precaution against a possible baroud. As for me, I am still in the bed of the oued, half hidden under a bush.

To-day is All Saints' Day. To-morrow, All Souls'. Mother, Jean, Jeannie, my aunt, &c., should be asking each other if it is my saint's day.

VI

SMARA

12.15.

Smara.

4 p.m. halt. (*At three miles from Smara,* 6 *p.m.*)

At ten o'clock the Aït Chogout returned : 3000 Reguibat and 2000 telamid (disciples), like flies, all round Smara. Nothing in the town, but a tribe might at any moment establish itself in the houses.

Hamper. Like a gum-drop, and a little more, to think that at any moment I should be face to face with Smara.

This land strewn with black stones. Here and there, bushes covering sandy stretches, where the 3000 Reguibat pasture their camels. The heavy burnous thrown back, I could see them about five hundred yards away, perhaps, over a distance of nearly three miles. Then there were only the stones which blackened the earth and the hillocks. Like the Ga'a desert.

Kept busy in my hamper by the bruises.

At the top of a rise in the ground, the Aït Chogout said, ' Look at the houses.'

Then I demanded my freedom. They refused, every one of them. I struggled in my bonds in the wicker-basket. They made the animal lie down. The Aït Chogout gave me a blow with his fist on my neck, and threatened my head.

208

' And if there are men ? '

Chibani, furious, blackguarded me. Furious myself, I said to him :

' Get out of the way ! Get out of the way !
(*Balek ! Balek !*) To hell with you (*Je me fous de toi !*) ! '

And, camera in hand, I walked towards the town.

A little below, in a treeless desert—and it was impressive, that terrible bareness, I could see nothing
clearly ; it was like a town in a mirage—were flat
roofs of the same colour as the earth on which I was
walking, and a cupola ; light yellow.

Three or four photographs.

A little farther away, the whole town appeared :
the two kasbahs, the mosque, the half-ruined houses,
and, the only greenery : palm-trees to the right along
the oued.

The Aït Chogout at my heels, shouting, forced
me to get into the hamper again, and it was thus that
I approached the town.

No walls ; the houses rise straight from the desert,
grouped round the large kasbah and the mosque.
Three hundred yards away, standing isolated on the
bare plain, the little kasbah.

The camels were pulled up among the first houses.
Taken out of my hamper, I went into a roofless house.
I took out my watch : it was a quarter-past twelve.
Immediately I wrote in my note-book : ' Smara :
12.15.' And at once I got the films, and a flask in
which to place the inscription, out of my baggage,
as well as the two cameras.

During this time, the Reguibat sheikh explored the
houses. Returned. Had seen no man. Immedi-

ately I went forward, harassed by the sheikhs, who feared that the Reguibat would come in force at any moment, and, without proper preparation, but phlegmatically, like a workman, I began the exploration of the town.

Those streets, trodden by men . . .
I thought of Caillié, in lively Timbuktu : mine was a dead city. The exhilaration which he must have felt !
But . . . how beautiful you must be, on your plinth, with the door of your great kasbah turned to the setting sun !

First the mosque, with its small cupola. I went in, followed by El Mahboul. . . .

November 2.
[6.45 *halt.*] *Seguiet el Hamra.*
. . . I saw its six bays, of which five were still standing, the two doors, the mihrab (pulpit), whose lighter facings were crumbling, and before it the hanging chin, which had lost its lustre of lamps. As I left, I found the stairway leading to the minaret. From that height the prayers went to the four corners of the Sahara, towards the tent-strewn desert.
I was too high, and too easily to be seen ; the sheikhs called me. The Aït Chogout indicated some camels on the plain, to the south. Chibani had taken up a place on the hills to the north, to keep watch in that direction.
I looked for a means of entering the large, square kasbah. I went round the walls, well-preserved, of

MICHEL VIEUCHANGE BEFORE SMARA

SMARA: THE GREAT KASBAH

SMARA FROM THE SOUTH-WEST

SMARA FROM THE EAST

SMARA: NORTH-EASTERLY FRONT

black stone taken from the desert. Four high wooden doors, with pointed arches and iron facings, all barricaded on the inside. On the arch of the western door, traces of green : the remains of inscriptions ? I was anxious to enter. But time pressed. I knew that sooner or later (although at first they said that they were agreeable to stay two days, and later changed it ·to eight the next morning) the sheikhs would suddenly want to go. I found a hole in the wall, which gave a view of the interior of the kasbah : standing on the back of El Mahboul, who was on all fours, I took two photographs, then went away, promising myself that I would return if I had time.

At that moment, I was on that front of Smara which faces south-west. A vast, desert plain stretched in front of her, a little below, because the town itself is built on a sort of rocky cliff eighteen or twenty feet high. Three hundred yards away, on the plain, isolated, stood the little kasbah. In spite of the shouts of the Reguibat, I had a mind to go there with El Mahboul. We climbed down from the cliff and began to run across the stony plain.

I turned back, however, and the town showed itself to me in its most impressive aspect, facing the desert which I trod ; desert herself.

We continued our march at the double towards the little kasbah, encountering as we went a cistern and two houses in ruins. Then we went round the little kasbah and entered. In the centre of the courtyard, bordered by buildings, stood a large round tower, in a good state of preservation.

Followed by El Mahboul, I went into the southerly building : floor of bare earth ; here and there stones

blackened by the fire.   In a corner, I deepened a hole,
and there, in a mint-alcohol flask, I put the inscription :

> [*My brother Jean Vieuchange and I, Michel Vieuchange,*
> *of French nationality, made the discovery of Smara*
> *in common, each undertaking one part of the work :*
> *my brother the task of coming to my aid should I,*
> *captive or wounded, summon him ; myself entering*
> *the oasis, November 1, One Thousand Nine Hundred*
> *and Thirty.*]

to which I fixed our two cards. (I remember the
difficulty in getting them through the neck of the bottle.
Time pressed : first Jean's card, then the rest.)   I
piled a little earth and some stones on the top.

My walk round the place, my search for the things
that ought to be photographed, were constantly
interrupted by the necessity of reloading the camera.
I did the same thing nine times : knife to open the
tin box ; film to extract, &c. ; number the boxes ;
describe each separate film, &c.

After the little kasbah, I turned to one of the ruined
houses and, sitting on the earth, opened my note-book,
took out my compass, and found the exact orientation,
then, with a few quick strokes of the pencil drew the
plan of the town. While I was doing this, strident
shouts from the Reguibat. El Mahboul replied that
we would come. I finished drawing the plan, and
we returned towards the town (photograph of the
town, of the oued with palm-trees, &c., of the cemetery
on a height above the oued).

The Reguibat, furious that we did not run back

to him, toppled down the cliff and ran towards us,
snatching away my camera as he waved his arms
about.

With the same gentleness, I took it back from him.

Soon afterwards, he had himself photographed with
me in front of the large kasbah, proffering his hand. I
don't know what was the matter with him—camels
approaching, men in sight, or something. We climbed
the cliff, at a place where there is a sort of winding
path. On the top, I turned towards the ruins of houses
lying to the west of the town. Returning to the large
kasbah and the mosque, we found Chibani, the Aït
Chogout, and the camels.

The Aït Chogout and Chibani wanted to leave
immediately. I asked for another moment (I could
feel that it was useless to try to make them stay till
sundown). Chibani was really terrified. He wandered about, gesticulating : no longer the same. I was
furious with El Mahboul, who insisted like the others ;
but, having a terrible thirst, I accepted a little water
from one of the lakes. I asked that the camels should
make the complete circuit of the town at a distance of
two hundred yards. The Reguibat preferred to go
with me ; the Aït Chogout sheikh to keep watch to the
south, Chibani to the north. The camels would be
driven towards the north.

I went at the double round the town, trying, as I
did for the western front and in the town itself, to
make a panorama (two or three photographs to be
joined together), particularly trying to include the
two kasbahs.

Going back in front of the cliff, I found the view
so wonderful that I retook a photograph. Then I

asked if I could go as far as the oued, to the palm-grove. The Reguibat sheikh agreed willingly. At that moment, he said that the baroud meant nothing to him. If I wanted to stay there five days he would be agreeable, &c.

We drew near the oued and began to climb to the cemetery which dominates it. Suddenly, shouts from Chibani. Immediately the Reguibat beat a retreat, worrying me. El Mahboul worried me : men arriving. In spite of the protests of El Mahboul and the sheikh, who had already taken flight, I took one last photograph, then followed them.

I caught sight of the Aït Chogout, who was making for the heights to the north at top speed. The Reguibat was already near the camels. He made the big camel lie down, untied the ropes, opened the hamper, and hurried me with his shouts. I had still time to look at my watch. It was three o'clock.

Without any care, with not so much as a burnous to soften the jolts, they tied me in the hamper.

I had not even time to throw one last glance towards the town.

* * *

Got together a few ideas on the march, to-night. Am trying to enlarge on them, as much as this beastly inability to think allows, but my intellectual machinery has turned everything upside down.

* * *

Here I am, having reached my goal.

Like the wing, who centres across the opposing team and puts the ball between the posts, like a stone from a catapult, I shot myself at Smara across a

SMARA: A CORNER OF THE GREAT KASBAH

SMARA: INTERIOR OF SMALL KASBAH

hundred and thirty miles of desert. And immediately,
as a pearl-diver hastens to regain the surface, seeking
to get myself clear of these savage places, I must turn
again to the north.

* * *

I have seen your two kasbahs and your ruined
mosque. I have seen you completely, seated on your
plinth, face to the desert, deserted in the silence, under
the glowing sun. I have seen your palms, to-day half
withered.

Truly, you are the work of man, of Ma el Aïnin at
the zenith of his power.

As if he had intended to astound the wandering
tribes by something miraculous, he established you on a
pedestal facing the setting sun, believing that thereby
he could give them some idea of his grandeur ; himself
alone among the stones, strong between the solid
masonry of the walls of his kasbahs, his subjects
everywhere around under the cover of their tents.

He gave a mosque to those men who wandered in
the Sahara, until that day having prayed only in the
wind of morning and evening, making their prostra-
tions as their route permitted, on rocks or sand.

And these men, never having seen a town, must
have looked on in amazement as the walls and kasbahs
and cupolas raised themselves up.

You, you had seen Marrakech and its buildings,
and, withdrawn into your desert, you would have your
walls and your mosque in the likeness of those of the
north. In the heart of your deserts you raised them,
lived there, drew there the unceasing migrations of your
Moors, that they might frequent your dwelling-place,

pray in the ten bays of your mosque, move to and fro
in the narrow streets. Now, when you are dead, the
tents are no longer near, drawn away in great eddies.
Your sons, not so strong (barred the doors of the great
kasbah ?), went north, to seek some reflection of your
power among gentler folk—and the Moors retain their
freedom. They look on with indifference as the walls
crumble and the cupolas cave in. According to the
chance of their journeys they invade your town, re-
storing for a few days, a few weeks, the noise of voices
and footsteps to the ruins, banishing the silence.

There, to-day, come their caravans of slaves and
arms. There they trade, and spread their merchandise.
I found spent cartridges, bits of clothing. There, in
your ruins, they light their evening fires and hold their
feasts, cooking bits of camel and of goat, whose bones,
horns, and hoofs I saw everywhere, littering the
earth.

Little they care, probably, for your buildings, your
mosque. Even your palm-trees they destroy. Not
one date. Still green, the first-comer rips off the
stalks and leaves nothing behind him.

You are of use to them only because there is some
shelter behind your crumbling walls, from which to
slay the enemy, because thanks to the advantage of
your position they see those who approach while they
are yet far distant in the desert.

Except for the nights when the fires light up your
walls, for the days when camels, goods, and men are
installed on your earth, how truly deserted you are
—town of the desert—how often your walls know only
the sun.

SMARA: EXTERIOR OF THE MOSQUE

Three hours only they permitted me to wander among your ruins—to be driven immediately far from your sight. And those three hours I could not spend in contemplation, nor could I wander as I would, nor for a moment rest ; running over you—like an anatomist—counting the bays of your mosque, distances, plotting the location of your buildings and their orientation.

On beholding you, and passing before that face which you offer to the setting sun, raising my eyes to you, without pausing on my way—my eyes on your great door that looks across the desert and dominates it from your plinth, like a vision which draws men to her, and behind which also they know is power—and as I passed under the dilapidated ceiling of your mosque, once holy and made for prayer, but which then I trod simply as one who came to see, I felt the sudden warmth in my breast, the response of my heart.

VII

THE RETURN JOURNEY

4.30 p.m. halt.
Close to the border of the two deserts of the Ga'a.

To continue the narrative :

We walked for ten minutes, reaching the side from which we saw Smara, when El Mahboul said to me through the burnous, ' *Arba argaz* ' (' Four men '). The Aït Chogout went to meet them. I heard the exchange of greetings : ' *Salaam*.' ' *Labès*,' &c. Voices very close for a while. Then I heard nothing more.

The Aït Chogout, retracing his steps, returned to Smara, where the others talked to him about the great kasbah, of arms (I am not quite sure).

We followed the route for about an hour. Worn out by the three hours in Smara : the fretting to which I was subjected ; the ' Dare I try my strength, and insist that they stay here, or come back at sunset ? ' ; the covering-up again ; the plan ; the inscription to bury ; ' Have I seen everything ? ' ; the disappointment of not having sunrise and sunset there ; ' Must I keep a roll of film ? ' ; ' I must go round the town again,' &c. — all that had wearied my brain. I wanted to do something more than simply make a list of the buildings : to rest my eyes for a long time on that horizon, on the houses and kasbahs ; let the stream, of which I felt only the first drops, flow in me.

. . . Unequal, like notes a little out of key, but presaging an inner working.

Some phrases came to me ; words that I would have written. And, besides all that, my body at the last gasp because of the race among the stones with my bruised feet.

At first, then, I let myself be put into the hamper, which suited me in the beginning almost better than the back of the animal. But very soon my bruises recurred ; foot almost dead, while my hand felt as though it belonged to somebody else ; thighs wedged ; the animal, driving off the flies, rubbed his muzzle exactly where my feet were : all that made my mind disordered, put an end to thought, to the birth of ideas. Impatiently I waited for the halt. I demanded it. And at last I got it ;. but the Reguibat refused to let me come out of the hamper. I submitted.

' Quickly—let somebody give me my note-book ! '

He refused. I asked El Mahboul to get it. He refused.

' The Arabs are coming back with the Aït Chogout, and they will see you writing.'

' Certainly not ! The burnous will not move. . . .'

El Mahboul refused abruptly, stating, perhaps to excuse himself, that the Reguibat had threatened to shoot him should he accede to my request—and left me in a frightful state. Shortly afterwards, the hamper fell from the side and I landed with my head among thorns. A mad rage ; disgust ; weariness, perhaps ; that crazy position, head lower than the feet ; the stones that I felt. I stayed so for two hours, until the men, who really had come back with the Aït Chogout, had drunk their tea and gone away. With a terrible

dismay I felt my head become confused : I was no
longer able to think about Smara, but only of my fury,
of my brain which would not function.

When El Mahboul appeared I cursed him. ' You
are no better than an Arab, and utterly worthless. . . .'

The brute laughed, laughed like a hyena. I threw
my slippers at his head. He laughed again.

I could not hold back my tears.

I put all this down because, here, I intend to enter
everything, absolutely sincerely. My sincerity in the
book will not be the same.

At that moment it was six o'clock. The sun had
gone down and the way promised to be long. I took
a little tea and opened the last tin of pineapple. El
Mahboul sat close to me. I was not sure that I should
give him some. I shared, simply not to make him
hostile towards me, and thought that he had not really
understood what he did in refusing me.

En route at seven o'clock. Moving north-east. I
was spent ; but I felt well. The cold wind whipped
my face and body. We came again to the black earth,
similar to the Ga'a desert.

In spite of everything, my work was accomplished.
I had performed my task. Soon I should see my own
people again. It was sweet to count the days to that
time.

Between the sheikhs, walking beside my camel, and
El Mahboul, also mounted, an argument broke out
suddenly. The Moors wanted to find the Reguibat
encampment, so that they could have meat to eat, and
stay there a day or two. Naturally, El Mahboul
refused. Having understood, I said that I would

never consent to it, that I would not follow them. I
had promised two goats and I would give them, but at
Tigilit, not here.

Near to some tents, whose fires could be made
out, the Aït Chogout decided to buy a goat, and went
off, followed by Chibani.

We kept on our way to the north-east with the
Reguibat, who turned towards me with a ' *Vieussange,
labès, labès ?* ' (' All right . . . all right ? ').

I could worry no longer. It was El Mahboul's
turn, who whined and prayed in a low voice to
Sidi Moussa. Perhaps they would return with some
men, and then we should never see Tiznit again, or
Mogador !

' But there is Chibani ! He will not betray us. . . .'

' *Man 'arf* (' I do not know ') : for money ! '

Halt in a oued. Waited half an hour, during which
time I kept the Reguibat busy with humbug and
nonsense : my brother who would come, &c. . . . the
tents . . . spoke Chleuh.

Ultimately Chibani and the Aït Chogout came back,
dragging a goat by the horns. Hoisted into a pannier.

We resumed our march. Crossed the two arms of the
Oued Gaïs.

I was absolutely frozen.

At 11.15 (?), Seguiet el Hamra. At midnight, halt
in the middle of the Seguiet.

Chibani spread the sugar-sack for me, and I slept
until morning, quite well bedded. Chibani could not
get over the fact that I had told him to go to hell,
but was a little afraid he might lose his extra reward.

In the morning, the march resumed. The Seguiet

is divided into two arms by a spur of black earth. We came to a halt in the middle of the second.

Slaughter of the goat. I busied myself editing what I had written, fairly satisfied with it. During the night, all the time that we pressed forward, in spite of the cold, thoughts germinated one by one, shaped themselves to my liking, brought me peace. I felt more content with what I had already put on to paper. It is not merely an inventory. I saw. I had been very much afraid that the abrupt examination could have left only a chaotic impression, a state of bewilderment.

Naturally, nothing is in proper shape yet, but it has movement, style ; an expression here and there which I feel is good. . . . I like these outlines : some parts nearly perfect, others still obscure.

Ate liver, grilled on a spit : I threw the intestines discreetly away.

Moved on again at half-past twelve.

Seguiet ended. Our outward route on the west. Clayey plain, then the black Ga'a ; mountainous, then level.

The sheikhs and Chibani were happy, throwing their rifles in the air, jumping, stamping their feet, singing of the meat and the return journey.

Two camels, worn out, refused to go farther.

The unending black Ga'a ; windy. I forced myself to keep going. Not for a moment was I without pain, my loins particularly, and my buttocks. But we moved north-east.

At half-past four came to a halt here, very near to the one we made the other day.

Monday, November 3.
6.30 *halt. Ga'a desert.*

The cold nights of the Sahara.

I suffer from the cold a great deal more than from the sun. Yesterday, having finished writing the above, shivering, I went to warm myself near the fires lit by the sheikhs and Chibani, one for the tea, one for the barley bread, one for the meat. Ate some goat, but hardly cooked, almost raw.

Lying with my head and shoulders resting on a pack-saddle, I suffered because of my feet, my stomach, and the cold (these cold nights of the Sahara). I had hardly two hours' sleep. Lice. After these two indispensable hours, I awoke. The same happens every night.

The moon almost full : the bushes. The two camels lying down, grumbling.

The sheikhs rose at midnight, but the young she-camel had disappeared. They hunted for her through the night and only returned at half-past three, and finally we got away.

The Reguibat sheikh, who stayed behind, lying down, will not rejoin us until we reach the yellow desert. We followed a road to the east of that taken on the outward journey, along the yellow desert ; but here it was still the black desert, where a little vegetation was to be found.

We halted at half-past six, to take a little tea and barley bread.

Three rifle shots were heard about two and a half miles away. The Aït Chogout could not help laughing

at the thought of his friend caught in an affair.   I did
not understand.

Written on camel-back, about 2 p.m.
Transcribed at the 3 o'clock halt.

We moved on again at seven o'clock.   El Mahboul
riding the female mehari with me.

We entered the yellow desert, whose magic circle
was complete around us.

The Aït Chogout sang in a high voice, which recalled the Moorish café at Oudjda, in the rampart
gardens.

Chibani and El Mahboul talked together with some
animation—Fatma Outana, the little horror.

Then, monotony and fatigue reduced them all to
silence.   The Reguibat sheikh rejoined us.

The powerful beast that carried El Mahboul and
me, and the Aït Chogout hanging on to its tail !

The clay earth—like pavement.   Dry lumps close
together, or touching smaller lumps, like a crocodile
skin, or scales, which cracked under the feet of the
camels.   Otherwise, the march was silent.   Their
wide pads tread the earth, whether hard or soft, as
though it were a carpet.   And there were only the
Eh's and the *Ah's* of the men to press the animals on.

Before, behind, on all sides of me, that infernal
line, for hours that were precisely the same, was
at the same distance away, bordered by the black
djebel which borrowed its shape.   The unblemished
circle, immutable as time.   Who watched it was
deceived, wearied as though by a will a thousand
times stronger.   It was better to look at the earth,
where the shadows moved little by little, turning, the

only things with life : or to consider the sick old mehari, his long neck flat ; his hump shrivelled —which had been God knows where !—his great eye under its strong bony arch ; his bloated skin ; his long pads and flabby thighs, and, like a fifth, the scrotum on which he rests when he sits ; and the saddle on his hump (he was not carrying it), which he wears like a crown : and to fume at his dismal tom-foolery, which drove him to come and squeeze my feet hard against the hamper.

Uncertain shapes, which I took for the clothing of a man, and which were the bones of a camel killed by fatigue.

Scorching sun, which branded me where the strap of the satchel lay round my shoulder. The walls of my throat stuck together.

Still I watched that line, to catch the moment when it would break, as I should have watched an over-hanging wave before it flooded the bridge of a founder-ing ship. Like the circumference of an overflowing vat.

Without any movement in the line, the djebel receded. A strip of black earth stretched between it and the yellow desert still locked in its magic circle.

At last there was a break ; the black earth in a gentle movement, like a sea, ate into it here and there, overlapping the yellow desert in places, breaking the infinity.

And very soon, the first spiny tufts appeared, to-wards which the camels moved immediately, necks outstretched.

We trod the black earth.

The Ga'a after [fifteen] hours' march was crossed : nearly [forty] miles without a drop of water.

Numerous camel-tracks ; drawn there, like us, by water.

Where the desert ends, the country of the baroud begins. The Reguibat went off, scouting ahead.

We had still an hour to go, before we reached water.

Water at last.

To-night, slept two hours, as I have recounted. From three a.m. up to now, we have marched without stopping, except the halt for half an hour mentioned above. Ankle beginning to swell ; loins ; head ; fever. I am not in very good condition.

Tuesday, November 4. 6 a.m. halt.

Yesterday, halted near to water at the foot of a rock. Green grass. Rewrote ' the desert ' written on camel-back. Delousing. I counted a hundred and fifteen pulsations : two quinine tablets. Meal of barley bread, goat-flesh (of which I drank the soup), tea. The sun went down. Romantic setting. Rocks, water, moon.

Resumed our journey. Nothing under my bottom. Angry with El Mahboul.

Towards eight o'clock, the camels refused to go farther. Halted in the valley of the Chebi. Wind. This time I slept until they awoke me—that is to say, for five hours. The delousing operation having been efficacious, I felt better. In pain, and all my bones cracking, I hoisted myself on to the big she-camel. She limped terribly.

At about six o'clock, halt. I went to sleep again while the sun was rising, and the sheikhs and Chibani lit a huge fire behind me to make tea. Then, while I wrote up the journey, &c., they attended to the camels. We started again at half-past seven.

Written on camel-back about 9 o'clock.
Transcribed at the 10.45 halt.

Prompted by a tooth which aches, and my feet :

In comfortable days, this fragile body which is of so much concern—our wealth—which one thinks of with humour, regret, or bitterness, because it breaks up : this tooth that will never be itself again ; this hair ; these furrows : this property, this fortune which diminishes daily.

Here it is merely the instrument of the thing to be done, and counts no more than for that, like the money for a purchase. And what is so gained cannot be dissipated, but is always in the coffers of our mortal experience.

The finest joys of life are born from this sensation of being in the essential verities, of growing rich in deeds, which makes for contentment as we look behind or ahead. One is no longer like a soap-bubble. We are strong in one thing and another. Even the deficiencies of the body are partners in the work to be accomplished, co-operating according to our intention, and they do not come on us like thieves, surprising us, attacking us, our money, and our rest in spite of all our precautions. This old, broken body still has its worth.

Same halt. Noon.

We followed the valley of the Oued Chebi, as on the outward journey. I saw the palm-tree and the hills again ; but they did not stand out as they did in the evening like the teeth of a saw, and the palm-leaves were dried. I felt no thrill ; time changes the face of things, and one trembles to think that if one had seen this or that at six o'clock rather than at twelve, there would have been a different impression : better ; not so good—who knows ?

Our route was not exactly the same as on the outward journey ; but we followed the valley of the Oued Chebi for a longer time. While they waited to fill a water-skin, El Mahboul raised a shout. Two yards away was a snake raising his head to strike, but which fled when he pelted it with stones. The Reguibat chased it, beating it on its head with a stick, stunning it, and killing it.

We came to a dead-end in the valley. Another valley opened on the right, which we ignored. Ascent of the hills, and the discovery of a vast panorama of plain and a background of mountains. All this country is called Aïdar.

Desert plain ; only a few bushes in spots. We rested in one of the clumps. The bushes, about two feet high, gave no shade, and the sun beat down mercilessly. Crows perched on the camels, pecking the lice embedded in their skin. The sheikhs had considerable trouble in finding enough wood to make a fire to cook the meat and make tea.

4.30 p.m. halt.

We travelled east across the plain seen from the djebel this morning, and which proved to be heavily daled. El Mahboul signalled to me that about forty-

five miles away (he said sixty, but I know his miles)
[to the east], we should find the place where our first
attempt ended.

Always the same soil, whose surface was covered
with myriads of black or tawny pebbles, which bestrew
it evenly (the same as in the black Ga'a) but without
a single heap. It is as though they had been sown
broadcast : a covering of the same thickness throughout, which gives the earth its colour. In places a
yellow earth shows where the seeding is not so close :
earth sometimes clayey, like that of the Ga'a, sometimes friable, which should, it would seem, make some
vegetation possible.

The halt in full sunlight having tired me and given
me a little fever, I was not likely to seem at the top of
my form. The sheikhs and Chibani looked at me
and shook their heads : sore feet, thin, pains here and
there ; that did not seem worth much to them, and
they told El Mahboul that I might well be bearing the
consequences of trespassing in the habitation of the
great marabout Ma el Aïnin. If that is so, then why
are the camels in the same state ?

These vapourings mean nothing to me, of course.
But I am afraid that one of them may get hurt, or fall
sick, and seek to find a reason. (Cf. the Reguibat,
during the first attempt, who wanted to blame me for
the Aït Chogout's bad foot.)

Along the journey through the dales I thought of
happy days. Then, but by what channel of thought I
arrived at it I do not know, I considered the rude life
of these thousands of people, nomads, or fixed tribes
like those at Tigilit, for whom barley is a luxury (its
cultivation prevented by the baroud), who live on

goats' milk and dates, with goat or camel flesh for their
great occasions.

About four o'clock, saw a mountain which strongly
resembled the one we saw on October 28, on the outward journey.   I wondered if it was the same, happy
to see the end of the journey.   Everything had come
into shape, fitted in so well.

I shall have explored a considerable breadth of
territory, it seems, through my routes not being exactly
the same, although not too far separated from each
other to prevent my locating each by reference to the
other.

At a quarter-past four, deep descent, with the bed of
an oued (Oued Aïdar) at the bottom, which flows into
the Chebi.   Halt for tea.

November 5.   10 o'clock halt.

On the way, I thought : Is it so great a misfortune
not to have seen Smara under the setting sun, not to
have sat among its ruins, not to have let my eyes rest
long on its horizons and its buildings ?   Perhaps not.
I do not feel inclined to imitate Chateaubriand in the
Roman Forum.   I did not come here for that.

* * *

My body : those things that once troubled me
greatly : the organs which did not function properly,
rounded shoulders. . . . Of no great moment here.

* * *

I hope there will be very few more halts ; few more
nights.   What increased significance these halts assume
for me now that there can be only one or two more

with the sheikhs : the division of the meat into five
portions ; the lottery of the meal. . . . like the last
cherries, the best, at the bottom of the jar.

* * *

The return : still more of this profound, wonderful
joy, coming from our lives—renewed, or rather driven
along a splendid road—of which I shall say nothing.
I dreamed, with what pleasure, of the hot bath I shall
have at once, at the very first moment ; of the first
meal, the first night. To have no more lice, never to
be too hot or too cold again. Sleep in a bed. Eat.
To find all that again after two hard months, the work
ended.

* * *

Travelled yesterday evening from half-past five to
half-past eight across fairly large dales. It was on this
march that I made the reflections I have put down ;
but I was not able to identify the guiding hill exactly,
and that spoiled the pleasure of our progress.

Abominable night : fever, sick pain in my stomach,
cold. Hardly slept. Always kept half-awake by
vermin. Terrible headache at four o'clock when it
was time to start.

It rained and blew, and it was a blinding rain : my
cloak was soaked, my bare feet frozen. I was hardly
covered by my rags : only a black tunic and the piece
of blue linen. The wind penetrated as it would.
Only my head, neck, mouth, and forehead were well
protected.

The moon, behind clouds, gave no light, and we
went blindly on in that frightful weather for an hour.
Then the sheikhs no longer knew where they were,

and halted again until daylight. They all lay down. Only the Reguibat gathered wood and made a large fire during the night, the sight of which comforted me again.

(Nothing to fear from the baroud here, it seems : too many encampments. A point to be considered—the zones of the baroud and of no baroud.)

He made tea, and called us.

Then we started again. Took the road always to the east of our outward route. That annoyed me a great deal : no more landmarks, and a country hard to understand when we marched through mountains which lay in all directions.

'Why are we not taking the same route ? ' I asked El Mahboul.

'. . . I do not know. Perhaps they are taking us near the encampments. . . .'

Two of the camels were all in and lay down every mile or so, although they had no burden. They spoke of leaving them where they were.

A little sun.

I have scamped this a little so that now I can get rid of a few lice.

4.30 p.m. halt.

The sun rose. Followed the valley which ended in a cul-de-sac. We climbed up at the end : new valley. During the climb, the young she-camel lay down and refused to get up again. They had to abandon her after taking off the pack-saddle.

I do not know why, but since morning the sheikhs have pressed on at increased speed, beating the poor beasts. I ought to say that once the animal was left in the valley the pace was a little easier. Full of suspicion. What were the sheikhs after?

They intend to leave us during the night, to go and find (or so they say) the money they buried during the first raid at the time of the baroud. And it is more than thirty miles away.

If they persist, I have agreed with El Mahboul that we shall not wait for them. More probably it is accomplices they want to inform. I am afraid of the Reguibat's legs. At all events, I have asked El Mahboul for three cartridges, in case Chibani should hesitate to use his gun . . . or if he also should prove to be an accomplice. All three of them are under suspicion.

The new valley which we followed is the bed of a river; dry, but still supplying moisture for a few bushes, and lying north-east. Obviously much frequented: numerous camel-tracks, made this morning.

At the moment when we came out on to a vast plain, which lay across our way, El Mahboul pointed out that, on our left, where I saw a small group of mountains, we ate a tin of fruit, and that before us was the range bordering the other side of the valley, whose far slopes we followed on the first raid.

Taken all together, this new route had one good point: it led between the two which I already knew, making it possible for me to complete and locate them in relation to each other.

The plain is not a pasturage. No tents, it seems, although the course of the oued is covered with bushes. A place of passage: therefore the place of the baroud.

A few minutes ago, a dog barked. Everybody rose

to their feet except me. Then the dog drew off, but
there must be men not far distant.

Thursday, November 6.
[8 *o'clock halt.*]

[Last night], struck camp at six o'clock. Plain
covered with round pebbles furrowed by a large
number of narrow tracks. Full moon. Wind.

I was on the big mehari. I watched the sheikhs.
They were a little to my right with Chibani. Suddenly,
without a word to me or El Mahboul, they left Chibani
and disappeared towards the south, avowing, said
El Mahboul, that they would catch up with us to-
morrow morning.

Chibani hurried the animals.

Why did the sheikhs go off in that fashion ? Did
they really want to find their money, or did they want
leisure in which to discover what to do—or not to do—
with me ?

The terrible Reguibat, I think, really felt the need
to break away from the little group, to go at speed,
to be free. In the end, it would be he whom they
would accuse of dealing with the roumi—and with
El Mahboul and Chibani also.

He needs these odd escapades. And besides, he
must be doubtful as to his proper conduct towards me.
He cannot think clearly when he is too near us. That
is why I felt it dangerous for him to go.

The other was simply afraid of his money, I think—
and perhaps he had some idea of finding the abandoned
camel and taking possession of it.

I should have liked to keep on with the march all
night ; but the camels . . .

Halted near to mountains in the plain. My nights are nearly all bad, propped against a pannier.

At four o'clock we continued, and, passing along the mountains to our right, entered into a narrower valley. To the left, hills separated from each other, each having its own peculiar shape : the first like a dome, the second trapezoid, the third a cone, or pyramidal. To the right, daylight was already in the sky. Among a group of hills, between two slopes : the rosy tint from which the day springs, and daylight flooded the whole earth ; but, to the left : a yellow moon still shining in the night ; a great orange moon between the cone and the trapezium of the two hills, almost at the level of the horizon, as if she had just rolled down the conical hill.

The camel which walked at my side seemed still to be in the night, with this great, distant moon beyond, while the earth on my right hand was in broad daylight. (I saw in that a marvellous setting for Bernard Shaw's *Caesar and Cleopatra*.)

On arriving at the foot of the conical hill (circled by bands of stone, like walls built by men, and which, of varying height, are also to be found on the neighbouring hills), vegetation suddenly appeared—palm-trees— and, some paces away, I saw tents and stakes in the light of the dawn. Immediately, I covered my face. We drew a little nearer : tents, with torn cloths ; remnants of fire ; framework of saddles ; basket-work : the baroud. They belonged to El Msiid (six miles away from the point where we had previously seen the settlement), the oasis destroyed by the baroud. For some fine palm-trees which still remained standing, other thick trunks, cut off about a yard above the soil,

with their strong scale, seemed designed to serve as
a stockade, without giving them the least actual
protection.

The oued and vegetation lay south-west. We went
north-east without delay, without even taking water,
because of the many people who pass this way.

We are at present in a valley with numerous bushes
(Aounekht : Aït Youssa), stealing along towards
Tigilit as quickly as possible.

The sheikhs had not rejoined us when we halted at
eight o'clock to eat, nor have they now, at ten o'clock,
when we are about to move on once more.

6 p.m. halt.

Started again at ten o'clock : valley between the
Ouargziz to the right and small range which we saw
on the way out to the left. Narrowing valley, in which
people do not travel usually, except in large numbers ;
in a caravan of three or four hundred men. We found
the camping-places : camel droppings, fragments of
blue linen, &c.

El Mahboul tells me that two or three men never
cross this way alone. If they came into contact with
an unfriendly tribe, their lot would be settled : escape
would be impossible. The Reguibat sheikh hoped
that we should not enter this passage without him,
but that we should wait.

Riding the camel all the time, on account of my
feet. In front of me in turn, Chibani and El Mahboul.
But, at the end of three hours, they got down, holding
their backs. Yet how many hours I have travelled
without descending ! Is there any wonder that I am
not fresh at the end of a stage ?

The old mehari, at the last gasp, lay down. It
seemed that we should have to abandon him ; they did
not want to wait. I got down, and gave him an
injection of oil of camphor ; six capsules : two needles.
Continued on our way very slowly. At five o'clock,
Chibani, who was ahead, came across a cistern. I
wanted to take a photograph, but Chibani asked me to
climb a hillock and keep a look-out. I watched the
camels drink, and then drank from the same trough ;
my lips : their lips.

Resumed our march. One or two hundred yards
farther on—water-hole. Then the tomb of a marabout.
I recognized, with El Mahboul, the place where we
came to a halt with the sheikhs, but could not find the
exact location of the ascent.

The plain widened before us and I saw the Mokto.

What a joy it is, when itineraries coincide, to compare them ; understand ; complete. And the joy of
knowing that we had certainly escaped the sheikhs—
had outdistanced the cut-throats—and were within a
day's journey of Tigilit, and seven or eight of Tiznit.

We dropped down into the plain. Fire, hidden
under flat stones.

Friday, November 7.
6.30 *halt. Oued Dra.*

This stage, I put the finishing touches to the
itinerary.

Last night on the other side of the Dra. Calm
night. Until nine o'clock discussed with El Mahboul.
We agreed to stay two days at Tigilit, to settle accounts,
&c. Lying down at nine o'clock, could not sleep a
wink. Rose at eleven. Full moon. And the cart-

ridge-case had disappeared . . . a jackal had carried
it off. Chibani hunted for it until midnight, and
finally found it . . . a hundred yards away.

Depart : stars giving me direction. The mehari
lay down, half-dead. We abandoned him after taking
off the saddle.

One camel out of three. Fifteen days' work ;
fifteen nights.

We dropped down into the plain. Interminable
crossing to the Dra. Several dried beds. At daybreak ; water. The moon still flooding the night
behind us. No sun : rosy glow to the east. Rosy
sand ; bumpy, with cracks. Slender branches of
shrubs. Delicacy. Winter scenery, almost. Hill of
heaped-up blue stone. Water dark-green in the dawn.
The she-camel throwing herself at food. We are
pushing on, fearful of the sheikhs.

11.30 *halt*.

Reached the other side of the valley. She-camel,
in turn, flattened out. Stopped at the beginning of
the Mokto. Chibani made bread ; tea. I climbed
up a rock to keep a look-out. El Mahboul has
annoyed me, thrown me into a rage. He seems to have
told Muhammed to be there only to-morrow or the
day after—and at that time we did not know we should
have a delay of five days.

Saturday, November 8. *Tigilit.*

We entered into the range, whose name changes
according to locality : now Mokto ; now Taoulikt
(Taoulikt is a peak), &c. The enormous ridges,
which one would have believed to be all of one piece,

proved to be extremely complicated in the interior. There was not only a range, but a group. The hills lay in all directions. That, however, is what made passage possible. We slipped between the enormous piles, sometimes cramped close together, at others separating into small valleys.

At the end was a climb, and sheer declivity that was really staggering. During the earlier raid I took my chances among these rocks in the dead of night ; rocks which often make stairways with steps two feet high, and are stiff, uphill work ; and escaped with my life. That accounts for the appalling weariness of my shrivelled arms as I hung on.

It was a little before we reached this crest that two shouts burst on us from the rear, in the ravine. I was chary of turning round, not knowing whether we had Moors to deal with or the two sheikhs. It was they, black with fatigue, coming along like moufflons ; magnificent. El Mahboul called to Chibani in a choked voice :

' *Ara* ! '

Chibani, who was ahead, stood for a good half-minute before replying, and then came near cautiously, gun in hand. The Reguibat opened his breech, and removed the cartridge, left his gun standing near a stone, and sat down several paces away.

Immediately, El Mahboul made the she-camel kneel, got out the kettle, and offered pieces of bread to the sheikhs, who ate them in silence, throwing dark looks our way.

' . . . Why did you not wait for us ? Why did you go ? '

I replied to the sheikhs :

' Chibani did the right thing.   Where I am ; he is.
You two went off, taking your guns, and if we fell into
the baroud—so much the worse for us ! '

What had they been up to ?   Had they been unable
to find anybody, or only too late ?

Chibani said he saw a troop in the distance towards
the Dra, as we came into the djebel.   Were they afraid,
so to invade the territory of the sheikh of Tigilit, or had
they really been to look for their money ?

We took up the march again.   Climbed up and
then began the descent, with me riding the camel.   At
twilight, however, Chibani took me in his arms, and I
came down, to continue on foot.

Wide horizon, but no sun.   However, I had photographed this mountain the first time I climbed it.

The she-camel came through these risky places with
an amazing sureness of foot—her long neck moving
from right to left ; raised, inquisitive head ; swelling
muscles below and behind the ears, which made her
look like a snake with its hood spread.

Below ; a succession of dales.   Rode the animal
with El Mahboul.   Sorry road.   Tigilit without Jean's
letters meant nothing to me.   Should I wait for them ?
Leave, like that ?   But men and beasts needed rest.

A strong wind rose, cold, and clouds covered the
sky.   Strange sensation, when cleaving an obscurity
full of jolts, of humps and hollows—trusting to something which moved under you, and hardly keeping
hold, sliding every moment to its neck, towards rocks
or earth.   I knew nothing, but nothing worried me,
because I was easier than I had been during the day.

Dismal and frozen, I found the way long.

Tigilit ; without news ! And I had been so happy about the return. Still, the thought was sweet that this time it actually was the *return*.

Tigilit in a nearby valley, where the wind dropped. While still a mile off, we dismounted, and the Reguibat sheikh went ahead to prepare the sheikh of Tigilit. Rain began to fall. Rolled in my cloak, I slept, disregarding the rain.

Roused by El Mahboul : a man from Tamanar had arrived with some letters, Muhammed was by the Noun with the baggage.

I could have embraced El Mahboul. I had not spoken to him since sunset.

The sheikh came to meet us. We shook hands. Young ; beardless ; thin ; congenial. He had had a bag of good dates brought to us. We could not enter the town immediately ; the houses were full of men of the neighbourhood eager to carry the baroud somewhere or other. They soon went, however, and after about an hour Lhassen came to take charge of me.

Frightful pebbly bed of the oued, which shattered my feet ; but, I was going to find those letters, which were to be the foretaste of the joy of our reunion.

Climbed the bank of the oued. Dogs barking. The rain had stopped. Palm-trees ; then : the houses.

I should like to have stayed awhile, to fix in my mind those poor walls which I shall never see again.

These places where men live ! I know nothing that is so moving. What are they like on the Volga, or in the Turkish villages, or among the fishermen of China ?

All these villages ; all these people.

Once more in Lhassen's house. There : a poor
specimen of a man, Muhammed's deputy.[1] My

[1] My brother let this messenger have the following letter :

' TIGILIT, *night of Friday 7th/Saturday 8th.*

' MY DEAR JEAN,—Here I am back again in Tigilit, this time
after succeeding. The joy I have just found in reading your
letter, and Jeannie's—an immense joy—because in spite of this
victory the struggle has been so hard every hour, every minute,
against my own fatigue, against the men, against El Mahboul's
lack of understanding (you will read of his uselessness at
Smara and on the way) ; that I have been depressed (understand
by that word : incapable of being joyous ; continually fretting ; if
you will) since I left Smara, excepting some moments when I
thought of you. Yet, your having been of the same will as I,
having sacrificed everything, as I, has been the only good thing,
the one which never has and never would let me go.

' Smara is a dead city, with a small number of houses and nearly
all the public buildings : a mosque, two kasbahs. The oasis is
half destroyed. Half ? Let us say three-quarters. . . .

' There is no question of its being a town, and the town of Ma
el Aïnin, born of his will in the heart of the desert.

' There is a periodic resurrection when the Moors invade it ;
their tents all around and a certain number of people in the stone
buildings. It is then that it regains some semblance of the days of
its fame. More people around it under canvas than in the town
itself, under the shelter of the stones.

' I saw it dead, at the moment when, most probably, life was
about to flow into it again. Five thousand tents, three thousand
belonging to the Reguibat, were standing a few kilometres away,
and one day or other, at any moment, might come nearer, and
the Moors invade the ruins, build their fires, cook their camel and
goat flesh in the alleys and the houses.

' I was driven away by the arrival of a body of men.

' I stayed there from noon to three o'clock on November 1 :
All Saints' Day. And I had to fight the sheikhs who pestered me,
Chibani and El Mahboul, in a raging temper but not losing one
second ; keen-witted (despite a little confusion at the beginning),
taking ten rolls of film, making an inventory, seeing everything

letters. Those of Jean, of Jeannie. By them my
pain—which I cannot describe—was slowly lessened.
My heart opened wide to joy.

except the interior of the large kasbah, which was barricaded on
the inside—and gripped, just the same, two or three times, by
what I saw : this town on a plinth of rock facing the Sahara—
a rush of blood to my cheeks, a warmth in my heart.

' I think that the photographs will be good. I am in five or
six. I send you a roll. In case of misadventure that can be the
film which bears witness . . . but I hope to give an account of
everything.

.   .   .   .   .   .

' It so happens that I have travelled three roads, so that I shall
bring back not only the survey of a single journey, but a real
map . . . at least, that is my hope.

' The chief thing, then, is accomplished. It only remains for
me to get back to Tiznit from Tigilit (two days " baroud " ;
two days Madani ; one day of easy-going. I will let you have
full details later). I think we shall be able to polish that off in
three days and three nights, which means that I am within six or
seven days of Tiznit and of our reunion.

' It depends to some extent on the camels. Of the three we
took, two have crashed on the way (which will give you some idea
of how hard it was—for men and beasts. Chibani and El
Mahboul are here in this room, sipping their tea ; half dead).
One single animal that made the trip remains ; amazing ; but
weary just the same, and another which El Mahboul bought (used
on the earlier raid) and which did not happen to be in Tigilit
at the time we were ready to start.

' I think that the return to Tiznit will happen between the
dates I have given you, and be without adventures ; that from
Smara to Tigilit has been rather eventful. Two days away from
here the two sheikhs left us to our own devices, under the pretext
of going to hunt for money they had buried ; but going, I believe,
towards accomplices who were to carry me off. Or, perhaps, it
was nothing more than a mad prank, another example of their
dangerous irresponsibility.

' They caught up with us again, all in, a few miles from Tigilit,

I am now out of Smara. I can see better what I
have done. The dross, the everlasting annoyances,

afraid, possibly, of the anger of the sheikh of Tigilit, and of the
baroud, not having found their accomplices. I shall never know.
Two days of flight, during which, at any moment, I expected to
see the Moors suddenly swooping down on us.

.   .   .   .

' All I have received are : your letter ; Jeannie's ; the pencils ;
the magnesium ; the hiatrine ; the quinine, brought by a man
from Tamanar.

' The remainder, including the money, is with Muhammed on
the Oued Noun. Muhammed may be ill, or the baroud raging.
I do not know exactly.

' The messenger leaves this morning for the Oued Noun, at
eight o'clock, and—either we arrange to meet Muhammed
half-way, or he may come on here. I think the journey to and
from the Oued Noun can be made in two days. I will tell you
that in a few hours (just now it is half-past three . . . I have had
something to eat, &c.).

' For two days the she-camel will rest, and the men as well.
As for myself, I should like to push on in an hour, a minute.

.   .   .   .

' I think we shall not meet at the Oued Massa, but about a mile
from Tiznit, on the track. Be somewhere near there. I shall
come along the track until I meet you. It should be about half-
past three, or four o'clock.

' Will you bring me some drug against the lice that are eating
me up ? Bring an old shirt, old clothes that, if necessary, we
could throw away. The first night I shall keep that old shirt. I
should like a hot bath as quickly as possible.

.   .   .   .

' 8 *a.m.*

' I am sending you five films, instead of one : numbers 24, 25,
26, 27, 31—all of Smara, and my note-book number 4.

' You should receive this letter on the 13th, and on Saturday
the 15th I should be about a mile and a half from Tiznit. Don't
worry too much if I am not there by Saturday.

' I have just been fighting like a madman with the sheikh and

fall to the ash-pit and leave only the fire. The journey has been made, and what was to be done is done.

We are carried forward, but she remains with us, our lovely conquest. Now she follows us ; captive. No longer are we the nervous hunters, calculating our possible measure of success ; already our eyes are searching here and there, seeking other captures to be made, other adventures to be undertaken, other conquests on which to throw ourselves. To-day we can assert ; exact ; scorn ; laugh ; cry like children ; take it easy ; live ! live ! !

Everything is good ; because of you, lovely thing, who, dead, raise yourself resplendent and incorruptible.

Sunday, November 9.
Tigilit. Morning.

During the night the sheikh of Tigilit summoned El Mahboul. He stated again that unless he gets an additional thousand or two thousand francs he will be

Chibani, who want to delay my start until the day after to-morrow on the excuse that the female mehari has a wounded foot, &c. This time El Mahboul stood by me.

' Till Saturday.

.   .   .   .

' MICHEL.

' I shall be at Tiznit, probably with four men—or five, perhaps some women. Buy mutton or goat's flesh, some good bread (not barley, I hope), and bring all that. They will make a feast. . . .

' Bring all the money you have with you, and the little revolver. Most probably I shall not have enough to pay them off, and there will be men accompanying me to collect the balance—and Chibani is different, becoming ill-tempered. I am suspicious.'

* * *

This message reached me at Mogador during the morning of November 14.

dissatisfied, taking it that he made a bad bargain. El Mahboul, as I had given him permission, promised three thousand, but not immediately ; at Tiznit. He told him also that the return was likely to be dangerous for me, particularly during the first few miles, because the rumour had said that there was a roumi at Tigilit looking for mines. If they knew of my passage, or where I was, I should be driven out and into the baroud. The sheikh of Tigilit has therefore decided to go with me, taking four or five men, among whom will be the Aït Chogout and Reguibat sheikhs, Lhassen, Ali, and Chibani, as far as the Oued Noun. There we should find Muhammed and his five thousand francs. The sheikh of Tigilit will be paid almost in full, the others will continue to Tiznit.

The route we are to take, El Mahboul explained, lies to the west of the one we came by.

* * *

Last night I put into order the specimens of flora that were scattered through my things. Of the rock specimens, the one which I picked up in the Mokto is there. All the others are lost (of the Ga'a chiefly). The others had been put into the hampers contrary to my instructions. Hampers broken, the specimens were strewn along the way. Some of them, from the Ga'a, ought to have been interesting, I believe. A miserable round pebble which Chibani picked up, and which I had put alongside the others, with some show, just to please him, is still there !

* * *

Having discarded my rags for the moment, and taken a large white tunic, new, never worn, I slept wonderfully. The night was mild. One of the best for two months.

* * *

The good she-camel is exhausted, poor beast, and I cannot make use of her for the return journey to Tiznit. Without her I should never have reached Smara, and I do not know how I should have regained Tigilit. The Reguibat offered me three hundred francs for her.

'You take her for a goat?' I said to him. 'If she cannot follow, then let her rest here until she is well, and unless somebody will give me a fair price, let her be brought to Tiznit.'

Of the three meharis which we used to reach Smara, not a single one remains at the moment. It will be necessary to hire others—if they are to be found. I have no idea what state the mehari we used on the first raid is in.

* * *

To be observed : the greater respect, the willingness to oblige, which grow in proportion to the nearer approach of the day when we shall separate. And this on the part of everybody : El Mahboul, Chibani, the sheikhs, Fatma Outana, &c.

This wretched room which I shall quit without regret, and never see again, where I must spend a few more hours, where I have lived in anticipation of departure, and of the thing to be done, recounting the obstacles, and the joys, to which I returned after reaching the goal, our goal ; only for a few more hours shall I be here.

I have spoken of its low ceiling, too low in places,

made of palm-branches and dried leaves ; of its walls, built of stones which protrude everywhere, bursting the already half-ruined plaster ; of the wall which divides it into two : one half dark, with no opening save a loophole ; the other, which gets a little light from the low door.

In the latter I am now sitting on the mat. Chibani, El Mahboul, Lhassen's wife and Taboucat, Bous and Fatma, sit around the tea-tray and tell each other confidences, argue, overbear each other, and sip their tea. El Mahboul officiates, and passes me my glass, which I drain with noisy gulps, after the fashion of my neighbours, and pass again to him to be refilled.

Behind the door is the brazier, over whose glowing coals Fatma Outana turns skewers on which have been spitted pieces of goat's liver and other offal, covered with grease. They pass me the wand, and I pull off my piece.

(I have already given them a goat : (1) to put them into a good humour, and (2) for the journey. It is incredible how a little grease makes things easier in this country.)

Strewn in disorder on the mat, so that it is impossible to put a foot down without treading on something, are burnouses ; turbans ; the sugar hamper ; the basin in which my bandages are soaking ; skin bags full of dates ; my camera ; my satchel ; my outspread maps, which I consult before departure ; my effects ; specimens of rock in their coarse linen bags, &c.

Taboucat shows me her little backside, watching every move Fatma makes, who passes her little bits of meat.

.   .   .   .

Monday, November 10.   *Tigilit.*

We did not start last night as had been arranged. I can no longer hope to be at our rendezvous.

El Mahboul was gone interminably long, during which I finished putting in order my baggage, studied the maps, deloused my rags by the light of a candle, and then lay down and slept.

His return roused me. I do not know what time it may have been. He began with an unending rigmarole in which he said I had—he had—not paid for the dates, three goats, &c. (I ? the sheikh ?). But whenever he has a nasty jolt to deliver, he always begins with some gibberish or other. I let that pass, and found out what was really the matter, which proved to be :

1. We could not leave during the night.

2. He had found himself in the midst of ten men, all aware of my presence (Ali the most implacable), all clamouring, ' " *Gib flous* " (' Give money '), or the roumi will not leave. Go and find it, we will take care of the roumi.'

From one of them :

' Your roumi is not American. He is a Frenchman. He isn't here about mines. He is studying the country, making ready for the French to come. He must not be allowed to go, not even for money.'

The sheikh of Tigilit, lukewarm, hesitating, obviously influenced by the tales of his acolytes : and I could see El Mahboul getting his head, talking like a windmill, smiting himself with his fist :

' The roumi is not a Frenchman. He hates them, and I, I would not help a Frenchman. But if he stays

here you will never smell a cent. You have seen the
machine he uses (my luminous compass) ? It is a
diamond ! At Oran that is worth fifteen or twenty
thousand francs. If the sheikh insists, we will leave
that as a pledge.'

I believe that he has also proposed his brother
Muhammed as hostage.

The sheikh of Tigilit, in spite of all this, showed himself still fairly friendly towards me. He decided that
they would take the road the following night (*this*
very night, then), and let us hope that that promise
will not be broken. But :

1. He will take the she-camel for four hundred
   francs, and
2. He will sell two meharis for fifteen hundred
   francs ;

and finally decided that I must change houses at once.

And so Ali came to fetch me. El Mahboul said :

' He will take you into his own house, which is more
comfortable than this. You will be all right.'

In fact, he took me and Chibani to the house that I
had seen once before, the one I lived in the first day
of our arrival at Tigilit, and which was later abandoned.

They made me go into one of the miserable rooms,
narrow ; but taking all the width of the house (that
will give an idea of the shape of the houses), and I
stretched out in the lousy (I am afraid) dust, my turban
under my head, my satchel at my side. When the two
men went, I slept.

When I awoke this morning, I saw a feeble light
which filtered through the holes of the low door, deep

at the other end of the room. I waited, heavy with
sleep.

Ultimately, at ten o'clock, Ali and Chibani brought
me some tea, and, in a cast-iron cauldron, some dates,
barley cakes, and the two kidneys of the goat, grilled.
They did not wait for me to finish before they went.

Lying around here : worn wicker-work, a sort of
wooden basin, and a plough that is exactly like those
of ancient Greece—I remember seeing a design on a
vase that was identical—a piece of bent wood, with a
handle on one side and, fastened to the wood on the
other side, a piece of iron.

I have drawn nearer to the door, to get a little
light.

During the whole time that Chibani and his nephew
were here they did not cease arguing and, as happens
now, I caught the general sense of their conversation.
It had to do with me ; the Oued Noun ; Tiznit. Ali,
the scoundrel, is eager to make me stay in his house
while El Mahboul goes to fetch the money. He also
hopes to eat goat at all his meals.

For myself, I have told El Mahboul that if things
drag on I should prefer to take the chance of decamping
to the djebel. It is not so difficult as all that. El
Mahboul knows the country well enough, and at
Goulimin and throughout the region he has friends
and relatives.

Besides which, he is an interested party, because,
if they were to separate us by force my plight would
not be too good. Chibani has, to say the least, rather
a doubtful attitude.

It is again the hour of solitude (ours, I always regard it), in which all the acts of solitude must be made good.

Afterwards, I will say : ' Would you be my assessors ? You shall be as armour, each one of you a weapon.'

. . . .

That is all we are, weapons. Death is familiar to me.

. . . .

Yet we are only on the threshold of solitude.

* * *

To describe the two mountains : The Ouargziz, sheer on one side, black, rectilinear crest : one cannot see at which point it can be climbed. The Mokto : fawn (light brown), sides lumpy, troughs of shadow, irregular crest with peaks (fantastic, shapes of animals, &c.) ; bare.

In the same way it is not easy to see at which point it could be climbed. In the passes it is possible to perceive the thickness of the range and all its variations, the ore, its intricacies and differing aspects. But it must be visited to be understood. The Ouargziz has no mystery.

* * *

Smara : the variations of the sterile earth, without a bush, without a tuft ; the stony ground and, behind a rise, little higher than the tops of dead walls which are hardly recognizable as walls from a distance of half a mile—men are so rare in that land of sun and stone and silence—some pedestals ; and, dominating all that, remote, unreal (giving a false note if you like) ; a little cupola, holed, canary yellow (light brown).

5 *o'clock*.

Have seen nobody since the moment when Chibani and Ali brought me the cauldron. I begin to be bored in this sort of goat-pen, where it is dark, where I begin to grow foul. I look out through the holes to the sides of the mountain lying north-east south-west. Clouds of locusts hovering. Not a sound. No sun. Weather heavy and cloudy. From time to time, human voices ; wailing calls of goatherds probably, near the oued.

* * *

Yet a little while, and I shall get a shot in my side.

Yet a little while, and a camel will bray and the djich, which is about a hundred yards away, will be on its feet.

Yet a little while, and the Moors will swoop round us and their guns begin to speak. . . .

These ' little whiles.' I have felt them in my marrow. These ' little whiles ' during which the face of things can change so much.

The other face. . . .

Like something poised, which falls.

In this insecurity, one feels something else close at hand, something which may break through, move everything, turn everything upside down.

It is a presence, very near : the sort of possibility which touches lightly on you, rakes your very spine.

It is in the air. Every second is ominous of the thing that soon will burst out.

Tuesday, November 11 (*night of* 10/11).
1 *o'clock in the morning*.

Compelled to wait, I was asleep. Some one entered

and called.   I awoke.   El Mahboul.   Match.   Candle.
I stood.

' We are going ? '

' They cannot find the camels ! '

I jumped on him.

' You are crazy !   What is the matter ? '

' I gave some money to a child to mind them.   He
went to get something to eat, and when he came back,
they were not there.'

' Why a child ?   Why not Lhassen ? '

' It was Ali who told me about the child.'

' Why did you not think about the camels before the
daylight had gone ? '

' I thought the child was looking after them.'

A little later, he said to me :

' To hell with the three camels.   There is still one
here.   Let us go, you and I.'

Then he wanted me to go back to Lhassen's house.

The fellow was uneasy, wanted to quit ; was ashamed
too.   There was a real to-do.   He floundered like
a child.   I sent him to look for my things.   He made
me lock myself in, fearful of I don't know what.

And that is how I was on the eve of departure !

8 *o'clock.*

Could not sleep.   At the end of my patience and
of my nerves.   I blackguarded him.   I roared and
groaned, cursed him ; but that did not help me at all.

He has been gone an hour, summoned by the sheikh.

Still, it would have been something to arrive at
Tiznit with three camels, Lhassen, Ali the cheat,
El Mahboul, Chibani, and the two sheikhs, whom I

hope to persuade to accompany us all the way. They have never seen Tiznit, never seen a motor-car. I was the first roumi they ever set eyes on.

Besides, to go with only one camel would give us away. I should run the tenfold risk of being recognized. But it looks as though I shall have to take the chance.

And again ; what of all our baggage ? We should crush the poor beast, and the men would have to walk all the way, never ride. How badly it is all arranged ! Is it an accident, or a plot ?

9.30.

All this cheating, more or less acknowledged, these revivals of antagonism on the part of the sheikhs, the looks of the Aït Chogout, like those of a wild animal, to whom I am a prey threatening to escape (he would gladly see me rot here, provided that I gave him goat, night and morning), make me find some satisfaction that I can reveal or not, as I like, their exact names [Merebbi Rebbo, knowing the sheikh accessory, would descend on the oasis and burn it. At least, that is one aspect of the possibilities]. And the haughty conceit of El Mahboul, his inconsistency. To-day, poor El Mahboul is a rag. It is nearly ten o'clock. Nearly three hours absent. Either he dare not return here or he prefers to sip tea. I do not know which. There is so much double-dealing among these dogs.

11.30.

About an hour and a half ago, Chibani came to tell me that the camels had been found. Left immediately

after I had told him to tell El Mahboul to come back
at once. And El Mahboul has not yet arrived !

6 o'clock, almost dark.

I slept a little. When I awoke, I heard the distant
braying of the camels : undoubtedly mine being
loaded. That ought to be the start, at last.

I had a weird dream, and on waking, my chest was
wet with sweat.

I was looking for Smara. I had reached a place,
to gain which it had been necessary to cross a vast, an
immense, an infinite forest. I went alone, with a
water-bottle, leaving my guides and baggage behind.
I knew that, ahead of me, some one else was looking
for the town. And it was Rene Caillié. I found his
tracks and joined him. I think he was with two
guides. He did not seem to be too pleased to find
me there. As for me, I was very happy, quite content
to share my entry into Smara with him.

Suddenly he said to me, showing me a peak in the
forest : ' Unless I had come across that, I should have
been dead, lost for a long time. . . . It served me as a
landmark.'

I understood that from that point he had travelled
by the stars. We took up our march again, and a
little later fell on Smara ; but oh ! what a strange
Smara !

It was a sort of quarry, cut off from the sky by a
peculiar network of threads, like spiders' webs, which
admitted only a little light.

(I remember that Caillié said to me, as we went
into the town, that he did not intend to stay long, and
I begged him to send me some magnesium wire which

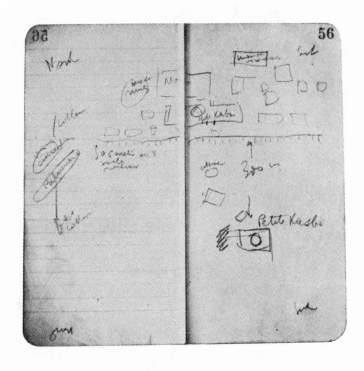

SKETCH PLAN OF SMARA
REPRODUCTION OF A PAGE OF THE JOURNAL

had been left behind in my baggage, so that I could light up the quarry.)

In the neighbourhood, some little excavations. I put my nose into one of them, about as high as my head, and saw something moving. Stretching out my hand, I grasped one of the inhabitants of Smara ; a repulsive little pygmy, who hung on to his place with his claws.

Immediately there were flutterings and rustlings around and above our heads. The air moved, and was full of this uncanny life, so that we were no longer able to see where we were.

What was more astonishing still for me was that, at that moment, the most abstruse words of Rimbaud sounded, and I understood them. And Caillié was Rimbaud. The words were spoken with such strength that if I had had my note-book at hand I could have written them down, when I awoke a moment later, with everything still fresh in my mind.

Night. Definitely night.

To tell of the three camels. Funeral oration on the young she-camel (how, at the halts, she used to put her head above mine, and wanted to eat my satchel). And the big female ; her buttocks, her slow movement, but what strength : all the baggage ; two men.

Wednesday, November 12.
3.30 *halt.* 7 *a.m.*

These mismanagements are so painful, so unending.

All the evening of the 11th, I saw nobody. I shall remember those two days spent in semi-darkness and

in absolute solitude.   A sort of pause, of contemplation,
before the last stage of the march, before the circle
rounded out.

It was dark, pitch black, without a gleam of moonlight (she rises late these nights) when Lhassen came
in, bringing me a little tea and telling me to get ready.
El Mahboul arrived a few moments later.   I asked
him why we had not started by daylight, as had been
agreed, since I had said I was willing to travel for some
miles in one of the hampers.

El Mahboul replied that a man had died, which had
made a crowd collect (of the people of Tigilit).   I
could not see in what way that could delay our
departure, since I should travel completely disguised.
Finally, since we were going to start, I did not rub it in.

We went out, and travelled about a hundred yards in
the dark.   Then El Mahboul made me sit down
among the rocks, and left me, saying that the Reguibat
would come to me and take me near to the camels,
about a mile farther on.

I waited nearly three hours among the rocks, anger
steadily rising against El Mahboul . . . one of those
rages that flood me, gnaw me.   There have been too
many days, too many hours when nothing has happened, when I have been kept in suspense.

I listened for noises—I could hardly use my eyes ;
all I could make out were the white sand, the sombre
mountains, and the slender light in the sky.   And
soon the sand grew dark, and then the sky.   Occasionally a few stars appeared and then were gone.

I heard a step behind me, about ten yards away.
Not the Reguibat.

Finally he arrived, accompanied by the sheikh of

Tigilit and the Aït Chogout. The sheikh of Tigilit, coming near to me, sat and said his interminable ' *Labès*.'

The three of them around me became very complimentary.

' You are a man ! Amazing (*mezian, mezian!*). You are strong ! Strong as an Arab . . . &c. . . .'

I replied with an equal flow of compliments. And we began to move.

The Aït Chogout walked at my side, very much the good fellow, affectionate, and took my hand, asked how many children I had. He confessed to seven . . . &c. . . . and asked me for a pair of field-glasses like those of the sheikh. The other two were just as amiable.

I admit that I was impressed, and said to myself that perhaps I had exaggerated their duplicity, that I should have to make a few retouches.

We sat in the bed of the oued, at a distance of about a mile and a half from Tigilit. The sheikh of Tigilit passed me a little bag made of braided reeds, full of dates. I thanked him, saying that I would send it to my mother . . . &c. . . .

' No, no ! Eat it now,' he said, opening it. ' I have given others to El Mahboul.'

Then we resumed our conversation.

' Tell your brother that at Tigilit he will be as though he were in his own home, that from there he can go to Tindouf, Smara, &c.'

The camels arrived, with El Mahboul, Chibani, Ali, Lhassen. They let the camels graze, and all the men gathered round and began one of those arguments that go on for days and nights.

El Mahboul, by my side, was uneasy.

He told me that at the last moment he had taken back the big she-camel and bought one other beast. I told him he had done very well. Then, in fragments, he told me that the sheikh of Tigilit refused to let Bous and Fatma Outana go, and would detain Muhammed when he reached Tigilit, until he had received every penny of his money ; that the Aït Chogout had behaved like a madman all day long, had done everything he could to keep me, the roumi, as a hostage, saying among other things :

' You, Ahmed, you are good. We know you. We are sure of you (he always speaks contrariwise, by force of habit), but the roumi is bad, he will give us nothing. Let us keep him as hostage.'

Finally, the sheikh of Tigilit contented himself with Bous, Fatma Outana, and Muhammed.

How is that for duplicity enough to make you laugh at your sudden accession of sentiment ?

The discovery restored my faith in myself. It gladdened my heart that they should be as I imagined them, as they had shown themselves during the journey ; but which, by an idiotic lapse at the last moment, I had begun to doubt, and was trying to gloss over, to make allowances for.

How good it is to be precise !

During the gossiping, they let the camels wander, and when they went to fetch them one was missing. They hunted for it for more than two hours, until half-past one, in vain. The Reguibat sheikh and Ali went back, and Chibani, Ali, Lhassen, El Mahboul, and I went on with the two that remained. The Reguibat will overtake us in the morning.

What a way to work ! It means nothing to them to travel thirty or forty miles to no purpose, to lose the whole of a day. The camels are always losing their way, because they have not yet got the habit of watching them properly. But that, also, is in their blood.

We followed a valley, or defile (I always hesitate as to which term to use), which wound to the north, to the east, to the north-east. Bushes and thorny shrubs. A slow march, lasting two hours.

At half-past three, we came to a halt. Mild night. Hindered from sleeping by my feet which, while they did not actually give me pain, worried me, and by a sort of white blister on the index finger of my left hand.

To-day, this morning, probably, Jean will receive my telegram ! ! [1]

Same halt. 2.30 p.m.

We have been in this valley for nearly twelve hours. The Reguibat and Ali have not joined us. It was understood that whether the camel was recovered or not, they should be with us at sunrise. I think of Saturday, at half-past three ; that is all I think of—of the rendezvous that I am certainly going to miss.

This inconsequential attitude, which divides us from these people, more than I had believed. This predominance of the present ; absolute ; mad. It is the mad desire to crowd everything into the day, into the moment. When I write, when I speak, it is true that I keep nothing back, but want to empty myself

[1] Muhammed's deputy, to whom my brother had given the text of the telegram, did not hand it in at the Agadir post office, but gave it to me with the third message.

completely ; but there does exist a continuity of design,
a form which takes shape of itself. Effort ; thought
which has a beginning, a centre, an end, a future, a
present, a past. They—these people—have only the
present, unformed and fragmentary. They create
nothing out of it beyond a few gestures, some ideas,
which are often at variance and soon fall to pieces.

The weather has been dull and heavy. Chibani,
Lhassen, are at the other side of the valley, making
bread. I hear the cracking of flat stones thrown into
a brushwood fire. There have been a few drops of
rain. The weather, still cloudy, grows cooler. El
Mahboul, who had climbed half-way up the mountain
to get a clear view down the valley, and at the same
time keep watch on the wanderings of the meharis,
is coming down to drink his tea.

Thursday, November 13.
[9 *o'clock halt*] 10 *o'clock.*

Yesterday, and to-day, a frightful enteritis, which has
almost finished me.

Yesterday, at half-past five in the evening, when the
light was almost gone, we saw the Aït Chogout coming
along in a violent hurry. We left again as soon as he
had joined us. He told us that the camel had not
been found . . . only the scattered baggage. And
its tracks, could I suggest ? The Reguibat and Ali
arrived very soon after. All they brought were some
things of Chibani's.

On our way. El Mahboul, on my advice, wanted
to leave Chibani's dates. He refused, obstinately.

Travelled until eight o'clock. Night too dark.
Halt. Tea in the night. We are seven. They feel

themselves strong. I was never so struck by the black blood of the Aït Chogout as when he was in the fire-light.

We moved on at [midnight]. Cloudy, and even a fine rain, through which the feeble moon could scarcely be seen. But the road through the valleys was not too bad.

About morning, we stopped again for an hour and a half. The earth was now very irregular. Everything was dry ; tufts burned up, no bushes.

At the halt, drew water from cistern, first seen since Tigilit. Chibani, lying down here and there during the march, lost our tracks. The Aït Chogout fired his musket. Soon afterwards the lost sheep returned.

At nine o'clock, halt. Valley opens facing black djebel ; steep sides ; big. Weather clearing. Photograph.

Stools—and stools—watery.

EPILOGUE

THERE my brother's notes end.[1]

    After his death I learned from his guide, Ahmed el Mahboul, what the last stages were like, as far as Tiznit.

Here is the tale he told, as interpreted by the caid Haddou :

The halt during which Michel wrote his last notes was broken at 11 o'clock.

They went by Zerzem, and at half-past one stopped at Tiflit Naït Skri.

There, for the first time after leaving Tigilit, Michel complained to El Mahboul of being ill. He made no notes but asked them to cook him a little barley-flour and water, and he drank a little tea.

At three o'clock they continued.

As they had been travelling through a district where the baroud is constant, they hurried their march. Michel maintained his seat on the camel with difficulty. Sometimes he called El Mahboul, who rode behind him and held him up.

So they arrived at ' the great north trail from the Oued Noun ' about seven o'clock in the evening. During a short halt of half an hour, while his guides regained their breath, Michel outlined again the route already covered : his last sketch.

About three o'clock in the morning, they refilled the water-skins at Fask, then hurried on to reach the quieter

---

[1] Michel always took up his narrative again at the 5 p.m. halt.

zone, under the sway of the caid Madani, beyond Tagant (Aït Ahmed).

Between Tagant and Bou Izakarn, they made a halt. It was nine a.m. The halt lasted until the beginning of the afternoon, and Michel, extremely fatigued, was able to rest in an empty house. The sheikhs and Chibani suggested fixing Michel in a *chouari* [1] so that he would not hinder their progress : the sheikhs being desirous of maintaining the utmost possible speed because they would be regarded with suspicion in the country over which the Madani ruled. Chibani, also, was jealous of the money paid to the sheikh of Tigilit, and never ceased to worry El Mahboul with questions and new demands : he wanted to know how much the Reguibat and the Aït Chogout had received, and to obtain a similar amount.

They restarted the march about two in the afternoon, reaching the forest of Agouni Imgharn, and during the night passed the Dhar el Akhsas, the residence of the caid Madani.

Some dogs began to bark. But Michel, who had ridden alone on the camel during this long stage of eleven hours, was so exhausted that he asked to be taken down.

It was one o'clock in the morning. El Mahboul, after removing to one side the stones which strewed the earth, spread out a little straw on which Michel lay. He told El Mahboul that he would no longer be able to keep his seat on the camel. He made the following stage in a *chouari*.

They passed in front of the souk El Akhsas, and made a halt a mile farther on, at about ten o'clock. Michel

---

[1] A sort of double pannier.

ate nothing, contenting himself with a little tea. But
the souk was thronged and the natives passed by in
numbers. Michel groaned occasionally under the
burnous with which El Mahboul had covered him,
and the sheikhs were compelled to distract the attention
of the passers-by with many *salaams* and *labès*.

They resumed their journey at one o'clock in the
afternoon, reaching the kasbah of Aït Larba el Akhsas
about three o'clock, and then coming to a halt to
make tea. The sheikhs and Chibani railed at Michel
and El Mahboul. Chibani was determined to take
Michel to the caid Madani and deliver him up. But
the sheikhs, fearing for themselves, refused.

Finally, the halt was broken after two hours' debate.
This time, Michel resumed his place on the camel and
El Mahboul rode behind him. They crossed Tasdermit
thus and reached Mierg. But the stage had completely
spent Michel : he could go no farther, and suffered
from the cold.

The sheikhs and Chibani agreed to halt, but would
not let El Mahboul light a fire. Since they were
within twelve miles of Talaint, Michel asked El Mahboul
to go to Tiznit to fetch a motor-car.

The sheikhs then became afraid. ' How is that
until now you have said, and the roumi too, that it
would be necessary to pass Tiznit without stopping,[1]
and now you want go there ? ' they said to El Mahboul.
They were uneasy, afraid for their money, suspecting an
ambush. ' It is a betrayal : he wants to take advantage
of the fact that we left our guns at El Akhsas.' [2]

[1] Michel having arranged to meet me on the track would not
stop at Tiznit.

[2] Before entering the French zone.

Chibani reproached the sheikhs for not having taken his advice ; if they had delivered Michel to the caid Madani they would have been able to share some of the ransom : in the morning El Mahboul and he would go to Tiznit, and ' as he is not American, but either Spanish or French, we shall not be paid. He makes us work for nothing : we must strangle him.'

Everybody was threatening. El Mahboul talked with them in turn, arguing, threatening the vengeance of the sheikh of Tigilit, and warned Michel.

What El Mahboul did not mention, but about which I learned from my brother himself at Tiznit, was the fit of anger with which he foiled this new treason of his guides, and was able once again to impose his will on them.

He decided, then, to make the last few miles which separated him from the French zone, on camel-back, and he mounted alone into the saddle.

They moved on. Stage of about ten or twelve miles to Reggada, where they halted. It was bitterly cold. Michel suffered because of it. El Mahboul covered him with his burnous. At that moment there were footsteps approaching : a man leading a mule loaded with wood.

' How much do you want for your wood ? ' asked El Mahboul.

' . . . 3.75 ' [Hassani francs].

El Mahboul bargained and got it for three francs.

Two fires were made. El Mahboul heated water for Michel, so that he might bathe his frozen feet. He also warmed some stones, which Michel held against himself. As day broke, they bought barley and eggs from some passing natives on their way to the souk at Tiznit. Michel took two glasses of tea and ate a little barley stew.

They moved on at about seven o'clock. Michel did not resume his turban, and El Mahboul asked why he did not cover his face.

' This,' Michel replied, ' is not the country of the Arabs.'

And then they met Muhammed who, instead of having reached the Noun as my brother thought, had stayed at Tiznit. He had with him the provisions which I had sent.

About a mile before reaching Tiznit, the sheikhs came to a halt on the side of the track, and Michel had a box of cherries opened, which Muhammed had brought. He ate a few with a little French bread.

Suddenly an automobile drew near on the track. Michel ordered El Mahboul to run to meet it. But it was a French officer on the way to Talaint.

Then Michel lay down and covered his face with his djellaba, to protect himself from the sun.

About one o'clock in the afternoon he scribbled this note :

> ' *Sunday*, 16 *November*. 1 *p.m.*
> *At one mile from Tiznit.*

' MY DEAR JEAN,— . . . for three days I have been murdered by a terrible dysentery. Please come as near as you possibly can to Tiznit (500 yards) without rousing attention. A mile has become a fearful task for me. MICHEL.

' Don't say that you are " M. Jean " my brother. And don't be taken in by the smiles of the Arabs. All of them except El Mahboul and his brother are hideous brigands. Believing me half dead, they wanted to strangle me last night, or take me to the Madani.

' I shall see you soon if you are there.'

He gave this note to Muhammed, and sent him ahead to explore the track.

They moved on again, passed by the gates of Tiznit and continued for about another two miles. The sheikhs and Chibani protested against going farther. They came to a standstill, took up their positions at a distance, and all the time they were making and drinking their tea, steadily insulted Michel and El Mahboul.

After having explored the track for two hours and a half, Muhammed returned, not having seen an automobile. As it was just about sun-down Michel then decided to return to Tiznit.

He received first-aid at the infirmary, and waited impatiently for my arrival. Risking everything, he telegraphed me at Mogador on the Monday.[1]

I found, in the note-book where he wrote the draft of that telegram, the following lines which I suppose were written at the same time :

> ' *These last heavy seconds, heavy as those when the flood is about to sweep away the bridge, like those when the miners working underground hear the sound of the pick below them, the sound of the counter-mine.*'

The previous evening, I, myself, had vainly searched the track in front of Tiznit until nightfall.

On Friday, November 14, the message which Michel had sent me from Tigilit relieving my fears, had gladdened me. And now, in this plain, bordered by the mountains of the Anti-Atlas, I saw the monotonous chains of caravans in front of the oasis, and the walls of

[1] I was beside my brother when the telegram was on its way to Mogador.

Tiznit. The words of the message sang in my head—
but, when I saw the sun on the point of setting, although
I knew well enough that half a day or a day seems
nothing at all to the Arabs, I could not resist the wave of
agony that swept over me.

I tried to persuade my two native guides to spend the
night in the open. But they refused obstinately,
saying that our long wait would appear suspicious,
and that we should be disturbed if we did not return
to Tiznit. As it was, the *mokhazni* [1] of the town came
to ask us what we were doing. We had taken off a
wheel, to give us a plausible excuse. . . . But I was
fearful of being driven back, or of losing my freedom
of movement, and I decided to go into the town, in-
tending to leave on the morrow as soon as the gates
were opened, knowing that if Michel should arrive
during the night and continue on the way to Agadir,
I should easily be able to overtake him.

During the evening, walking through the souks, I
suddenly saw Muhammed. Then he had not gone to
the Noun ! In my amazement, I let him get away and
lose himself in the throng. For a long time I looked
for him in the souks, among the kif-smokers, in the
fonduks, and in the dark alleys. If he had recognized
me, why should he hide ? He had not looked ill.
Was he stealing the five thousand francs I had en-
trusted to him ? [2]

At the break of day, we left Tiznit. I hunted along
the banks of the Oued Massa and in vain scrutinized
all the groups of natives that we passed on the way back
to Agadir.

The   missed   rendezvous,   the   meeting   with
[1] Mounted soldier or policeman.   [2] See note, p. 141.

Muhammed, threw me into apprehension. What was at the bottom of the delay, this presence of Muhammed in Tiznit ? I decided to go to Mogador, and to return to Tiznit, accompanied by a native who should keep a look-out on the trail when it was necessary.

When, on Monday evening, I again appeared at the bureau of information at Tiznit, the lieutenant of the garrison cut short my explanations, telling me that my brother was there. And he took me through a labyrinth of red walls and courtyards burned by the sun. Nothing could restrain my joy. I understood that Michel was in the infirmary with a touch of dysentery, but I was not uneasy.

How my joy increased the tragedy of the reunion !

The picture of Michel tore me brutally, broke me completely, choked even the flow of my tears. I felt a terrible fear sweep over me, even though I could not deny a sense of happiness.

Throughout the night I watched over Michel. Conversation was interrupted from time to time by brief snatches of sleep. He told me of the feverish hours at Smara, the miles travelled in the *chouari*, the treachery of Chibani and the sheikhs, the contemptible conduct of El Mahboul at Smara, but also of his faithfulness. He asked me what I thought of his notes, his photographs. And above all, he told me what I had meant to him during the raid.

In the morning, the aeroplane that was to take us to Agadir [1] descended at Tiznit.

[1] This aeroplane was generously placed at Michel's disposal by the Compagnie Générale Aéropostale, whom I thank most warmly, as I do also M. Baïle, the pilot.

What hidden conflict took place in Michel in the fearful noise of the aeroplane ; during the long hours of waiting in the stretcher at Agadir under the hangar ; during the painful ascent to the kasbah, punctuated by halts, his whole body shattered by the jerks of the truck ? What hidden conflict while receiving first-aid during the first night spent in the poor room of the hospital, during the first long day ?

Spent by the journey, he could not speak much to me. As for me, I had no other thought but to watch over him, alone, until the devotion of the nurse, Mlle Gabrielle, came to my support.

The second night Michel called me, and spoke to me as he had never done before.

In his mouth, what new significance the words had ! I realized that we were to abandon the plane on which we had lived up to that time. Very simply, he confessed his complete acceptance of the Catholic faith— ' like Claudel,' he said. And he sent for the chaplain.

After such a return to the faith, while Michel never ceased to suffer, and although the end remained in doubt, a great peace possessed him : without relinquishing for a moment the fight against his illness, he was able to face death with serenity and even with joy.

During the evening of November 29, Michel once more dictated to me the text of a telegram to our parents . . . the last.

My brother died during the morning of the 30th, after a short agony.

APPENDIX

MY brother had no thought of publishing these journals; they were intended simply to refresh his memory. The book which he planned to write on his return would have been entirely different.

I have simply tried to facilitate the reading of the journals, interfering as little as possible with the original matter.

I have added here and there an article or pronoun omitted on account of the speed at which the writing was done—additions so minute that I have not marked them, since they alter neither the thought nor the style.

On the other hand, the nouns interpolated are placed between square brackets. Place-names enclosed in square brackets in the text are those which were indicated by Michel, either in the margin of the text or in the sketches of his itineraries. The names of places given in footnotes are those supplied by the guides, when interrogated by the caid Haddou.

I have extracted some passages from the letters sent to me by Michel, and introduced them into the narrative, in order to make it clearer. They are placed in square brackets. For better understanding, I have substituted the time of the halt for the actual time of writing.

I have suppressed certain passages: particularly some rough drafts, unfinished soliloquies which were too fragmentary, and thoughts concerning our future activities (it would have been too painful to me to let anything of my personality intervene in plans which could only have been realized together). The omissions are indicated by points or a line of points.

INDEX